With Very Best
John B

Keeping Your Sense of Tumour

My fight against myeloma, pneumonia, septic shock,
chest infections, shingles – and an ingrowing toenail!!!

– JOHN BLACKBURN –

An environmentally friendly book printed and bound in England by
www.printondemand-worldwide.com

Mixed Sources
Product group from well-managed
forests, and other controlled sources
www.fsc.org Cert no. TT-COC-002641
© 1996 Forest Stewardship Council
FSC

PEFC
PEFC/16-33-415

PEFC Certified
This product is
from sustainably
managed forests
and controlled
sources
www.pefc.org

This book is made entirely of chain-of-custody materials

www.fast-print.net/store.php

Keeping Your Sense of Tumour
Copyright © John Blackburn 2012

ISBN 978-178035-298-5

First published 2012 by
FASTPRINT PUBLISHING
Peterborough, England.

Dedication

As this may well be the only 'proper' book which I ever succeed in completing, by which I mean not counting the 'Ave Maria' mini-book currently available as a download for Kindles via the Amazon website (plug, plug!), I would ask you to bear with me as I take the opportunity to spend a little time over this dedication. I would like to spread it as wide as I can as there are so many people I need to thank for both extending my life and giving it a quality it might not otherwise have had.

Top of the list has to be my wife Su who has been with me every step of the way for nearly forty years now and has done almost everything for me especially over the last few years. I couldn't have got through all this without her and she deserves any plaudits which may ever come her way along with my undying gratitude and love.

Then there's the rest of my immediate family – grown-up children Christopher and Rachael along with their 'other halves' Alison and Dave. Su and I are very proud of our children and they have both proved time after time that we must have done a good job bringing them up! In addition Christopher and Alison have presented us with our first grandchild, and Charlie has been an absolute delight from the word 'go'!

My own family has been incredibly supportive too. My oldest brother Bob set me a wonderful example as he battled cancer for two years before sadly succumbing to it while I was in hospital. Alan, just a year older than my twin sister Barbara and me, has been a most regular visitor, advisor, taxi driver and supplier of liquid refreshment and other presents. Barbara has probably suffered with me more than most, but whether that's because of the empathy which exists between twins or the fact that she has had health problems of her own throughout her life so understands what it's all about I don't know, but she's always made sure she's around when needed and I couldn't possibly ever forget the number of times she brought me my KFC and various pies while I was struggling to eat Cuerden Grange's own food!

My in-laws shouldn't be overlooked either – Bob's family and Alan's and Barbara's, plus Su's sister Chris all deserve honourable mention with Chris being a constant support for us despite living nearly 200 miles away. Her regular visits throughout 2009 meant that knowing she was staying with Su during much of my time away was a constant source of reassurance for me.

Many friends, fellow football supporters, work colleagues and neighbours have helped with their prayers, cards, letters, text messages and good wishes and where would I have been without the incredible work done by Dr. Sture at the Ryan Medical Centre, so many people at Royal Preston Hospital and later the staff of Cuerden Grange? I do feel, though, that I should single one other person out, and that is my oldest friend, Ian Hyde. After everything he has done for us in the time since my illness was diagnosed, he himself is now battling cancer. At the time of writing he has just about finished his treatment and is recuperating slowly but surely and everything has been positive so far. I hope he continues to improve and makes a full recovery because he really does deserve it!

Last but definitely not least I must thank my media contacts – Chris Maguire, Charlotte and everyone else at the Chorley Guardian; Aasma Day, Peter Richardson and their colleagues at the Lancashire Evening Post; Paul O'Gorman and Sean McGinty at Radio Lancashire. All of you have helped to make this possible and brought it to the attention of so many people. Oh yes, and thanks too to Paul Swarbrick for permission to use his photograph of Christopher and Alison's wedding. Finally, thanks to Pauline, Marika and everyone else at Fast-Print Publishing who have been responsible for the actual production of the book.

I owe you all so much and you have my eternal gratitude, it has been heart-warming to realise how many real friends I've got, but if anyone reading this feels left out I'm sorry, please accept my humble apologies. God bless you all!

John Blackburn

Contents

Introduction

You can never know how you're going to react when told that you've got an illness as serious as cancer until it happens to you. It has become such an emotive word that its very mention brings a chill to the bone. I thought it was bad enough when I heard that my oldest brother Bob had been diagnosed with it eighteen months earlier, plus a false alarm for my brother-in-law Ray shortly after, but for it to raise its ugly head in me was even more of a bombshell. I had always thought that if confronted by such a scenario I would have crumbled, crawled into a corner and waited for the inevitable end. But I didn't – I don't know where the strength to cope came from or how I managed to do it, but the truth is that against the odds the biggest coward in the world is still here and battling more than three years after being given the earth-shattering news that not only had I got a tumour on my spine, but also I was suffering from multiple myeloma, cancer of the bone marrow, a disease which I was told though not curable, is at least treatable. I also contracted pneumonia and septic shock while in hospital, which proved to be almost fatal, and while being treated for that in the coronary care unit I learned that Bob had passed away.

My troubles didn't end after I'd left hospital either – I moved into a nursing-home to continue my rehabilitation and while there I had a bad chest infection and a serious dose of shingles. Even now, more than two years later, the after-effects of the shingles are still with me, a condition known as post-herpetic neuralgia, though I find it much easier to call it the "Shingle Tingle", which describes it quite accurately as far as I am concerned!

Many people before me have had what I've got and far worse too, and there'll be many more after me as well, so my story is far from unique. The example of many of those who've gone before has helped me enormously, and in particular for me that means Bob, and I would like to think that telling my story might possibly be of some small help to others in the future.

Many years ago Pat Seed grabbed the public imagination with her "One in a million" badges, while the inspiration given by Jane Tomlinson continuing with her gruelling sports events despite her condition touched many a heart. Nigella Lawson's late husband John Diamond set a good example for the likes of me when he subtitled his story "Because Cowards Get Cancer Too"! Closer to home for me, a few years ago an ex-Mayoress of Chorley, Mary Wilson, with the help of her local paper the Chorley Guardian, launched a fund called Mary's Prayer and that had raised more than £50,000 by the time she lost her battle with cancer in 2008.

You can see where this is going now, can't you? It is my hope through this little book to raise funds for a variety of cancer-related charities, both local and national, given the nature of my condition and hence the subject matter in these pages.

Any profits which we may be fortunate enough to make will go straight to appropriate charities, but I hope that we may be able to persuade people to contribute whatever they can afford whether they buy a copy or not so that we can raise as much as possible before I go a-clog-popping, and even after for that matter! Meanwhile, we'll just take each day on its merits and hope that there are still quite a lot of them to go yet…!

I would also be most interested to receive any feedback from anyone who may wish to get in touch especially as a consequence of reading the book. I fear, however, that I have resisted all attempts to persuade me to go on Facebook, Twitter or any other of the social networking sites but I can at least be contacted by email, and for this my address is johnblackburn@blueyonder.co.uk. I look forward to hearing from you – I think!

Part 1 – Hospital

Chapter 1

"It's A Bit Of A Bugger This, Isn't It?!"

I'd had a touch of backache almost throughout 2008, but typically didn't do anything about it till it seriously started to affect various aspects of my life. I didn't take time off work with it, but as it started to get worse I had to get others to lift things for me. Being a hypochondriac by profession, but a devout coward by religion, I was used to frequently feeling ill, but never doing anything about my many 'ailments'. This, though, was turning into something more serious, so in September I decided it was time to go to the doctor's with it, still wondering whether I would be told that the only thing wrong with my back was the big yellow streak running right through it! In the event I was prescribed painkillers and sent to hospital for an x-ray, which didn't show up anything abnormal. In itself, of course, this was good news but didn't help to solve the problem. The doctor wanted me to have blood tests too but I was reluctant to go down that road because of a lifelong phobia about needles. My mobility gradually became very restricted and the pain in my back started to get worse, the only significant relief coming from soaking in a hot bath. As my condition deteriorated I needed to use a walking-stick to get about and though I went to work as usual on December 19th 2008 I had forgotten to take my painkillers with me, so I decided to come home at lunchtime to get them. I never went back!

A major restructure had started to take place at work and the department in which I worked was being abolished, so we were all going to have to seek new jobs, though still roughly in the same type of work. None of us were very happy about this, and I decided that after forty-three years it was time to call it a day. My wife, Su, and I had done our arithmetic and worked out that with the lump sum I would get as a result plus my occupational pension we could probably manage, even if there would be another four years before I would get my state pension. Accordingly I had already handed in my notice a month before my illness came to a head. Financially my timing was clearly not very good as it turned out but I wasn't to know that at the time.

I just about managed to drive to our doctors' surgery, the Ryan Medical Centre, on Tuesday the 23rd of December with Su for company and Dr. Sture, who had been treating me all along, was most concerned by the downturn in my condition since our last meeting, as a result of which she told me to go straight back home and said that she would arrange for an ambulance to come to our house and take me to hospital. Fortunately the doctor's is only about half a mile from our home and I succeeded in getting us back home without harming either us or any other unwitting road users or pedestrians, but strictly speaking I don't think I should have been driving even that short distance, such were my limitations by that stage. Let's put it this way – I have never driven since!

What happened that afternoon seems so strange now that I would be wondering if I had possibly dreamt it all up were it not for the fact that Su went with me and can confirm that this is what really took place. I was seen after a while by a Dr.Kelly who made me walk up and down the ward, then he stuck his finger up my bum and sent me home! That's what it amounted to anyway – he asked me a number of questions as well, but his conclusion from what evidence he gleaned as a result of my answers and his observations was that the problem was neurological so I should go home and wait for an appointment with a neurologist as was already being arranged by my GP. I'm not sure quite why he felt it necessary to include an anal inspection too but in situations like that "ours not to reason why…!" Well, I think he was a doctor, he was wearing a white coat and carrying a clipboard, but sometimes when I think about it I wonder…

We stumbled through Christmas, or to be more accurate I stumbled and Su kept me on my feet as best as she could, but once I went upstairs on Boxing Day it was clear that I wouldn't be going back down under my own steam, having by that time completely lost the use of my right leg. The sight of Su wheeling me to and from the bathroom on a computer chair might have raised many an eyebrow had we been on view! She rang the surgery on the Monday morning following Christmas (the 29th), and this was the day we were supposed to be socialising with the rest of the family at my brother Alan's house. Instead he came to us and brought me a few cans of beer, and I think he was quite taken aback to see the condition I was in. Doctor Sture called and immediately sent for the ambulance and before I knew it two burly paramedics were struggling to get me downstairs in one of their chairs to start me off on the journey to hospital. Little did I know then but it would be just one week short of a year before I would come back to sleep under my own roof again!

The rest of that day is something of a blur, certainly as far as what happened when is concerned, but there are parts of it which will remain with me for ever. Anyone who's undergone an MRI scan isn't likely to forget it, but I had other tests too – x-rays and blood tests for instance, and these would become regular experiences for me throughout my five months in hospital. The first of those blood tests led to my worst fears being realised – I passed out within a couple of minutes of it being taken! It was what I had always expected would happen if I had one, so I probably willed it on myself without realising it. Fortunately that was the only time it has happened and I've had rather a lot of blood tests since, and well over a thousand other injections too, but occasionally I still get a bit 'queasy' when it's being done, or shortly after.

Once they had completed that initial round of tests, it was time to deliver their verdict – and what a verdict it was! Su was given the diagnosis by the doctor who had first admitted me, but I don't know who the guy was who told me. All I can say is that Su and Christopher came in part way through his speech, so they were able to see my response first-hand. Su had managed to get news to Christopher about what was going on so he was diverted from his original journey en route to a football match. The gist of the diagnosis was that they had found a tumour on my spine which was pressing on my spinal cord and that was the reason that I'd lost the use of my right leg. It was important, he said, that they operated as soon as possible to move or remove it if there was going to be a chance of me ever walking again. In addition, he told me that this tumour was a secondary cancer, and they would have to undergo further tests to determine where the primary one was. Only then could they decide what would be the best treatment for me. Having delivered his verdict, he then left us to come to terms as best as we could with the earth-shattering news. There wasn't really much any of us could say, but Su tells me that I was the one who broke the silence by uttering the phrase which is the heading of this chapter. It was actually a variation of what my late father-in-law had said to me a few months before he died back in 2002. He had been to the latest of a succession of funerals of his contemporaries and his parting shot to me that night as I dropped him off at his home was "They're a bit of a bugger these funerals, aren't they?!" It summed it up for him then and it was the same for me that night after my diagnosis. We all went quiet again after that and further words were few and far between. I think their thoughts were mainly focussed on what my reaction was going to be, then they could take their lead off me. For my part, words seemed to be empty, there wasn't much I could think of which would merit sharing with them once I'd given them my initial summing-up. With hindsight, we think there was an element of us all trying to put on as brave a face as possible for the sake of each other. The next few days would help us to clarify our thoughts, especially once the operation was out of the way and the full diagnosis became known.

Before the evening was over, however, I still managed to shock them both. There had been long periods of silence as we struggled to find anything appropriate to say, and most of the time was spent with us deep in our own thoughts. One phrase, though, kept nagging away at me, and eventually I felt compelled to share it with my visitors. I've always been a fan of word-play and puns, so it wasn't entirely unusual for me at that point to tell them that if ever I got round to writing about what was happening I would have to say that at a time like this it's important that you don't lose your sense of tumour! The silence which followed this admittedly dreadful pun you could have cut with a knife, and the sight of jaws dropping had to be seen to be believed, but then a smile appeared, and then another, but at least the cries of "Dad!!!" and "John!!!" when they arrived were accompanied by smiles and the solemnity which had pervaded the atmosphere was at least temporarily dispelled. I think the outcome was that they felt they would be able to leave me without worrying too much how I would be overnight, though of course the cold light of day would bring its own problems. The phrase itself has of course now found a life of its own as the title of this book!

And then they went and I was suddenly alone with my thoughts. How long could I realistically hope to have left? Could it be counted in months or years or would that be too optimistic? Where were they going to find that the primary cancer was? It's only when confronted like that that you realise there are an awful lot of possible places where it could be and, surprise surprise, I didn't fancy any of them! Worse still, I seemed to be able to make a case for each one as it came to mind – liver, bowels, prostate, throat, etc. Wherever it was going to be, it didn't paint a very pretty picture. What I didn't know at the time was that I had been given a bit of misinformation earlier, there wasn't a primary and secondary cancer, both were part of the same, Still, in my eyes all I could think was that I was lumbered, and this time there could be no running away. I must have dozed off eventually, but it wasn't long before I was awake and having to face the same questions all over again. Having said that, though, "sufficient for the day is the evil thereof", and there was no point worrying about anything else till I'd got over the operation which I knew was going to take place sooner rather than later. I was given the news early on Tuesday that it was going to be the following day, which happened to be New Year's Eve. Having seen the New Year in the previous two years at a concert at the Guild Hall in Preston, we would have probably done the same again that year had it not been for my condition, yet lo and behold I was going to see 2009 in at a theatre in Preston after all, though perhaps not the kind of theatre I would ideally have chosen! I was moved out of the neurological ward 17 to which I had originally been admitted into a little room of my own in a surgical ward in preparation for my op. I would be moved around that ward and the one next to it in the days following my surgery, wherever they felt I should be. There was a clock on the wall facing me in that first room, so the next day and a half I spent clock-watching right up to the time they came to take me to theatre. I'd no desire to read or watch telly. As is my wont when faced with personal crises, I just wanted to be left on my own with my thoughts. I didn't particularly want company apart from my closest family nor did I want anything else to intrude into my little world. And this went on right through until they came to get me, which wasn't until early evening on the Wednesday. Had I not been in hospital I would have been at the pub on the Tuesday evening drinking the health of two friends from work who were also leaving the library service in Chorley, one for early retirement the other for promotion elsewhere in the county. I can remember lying there looking at the clock and thinking how much I'd rather be there with them than where I was, and I heard later that it was rather a subdued gathering that night as they had all been informed of my situation at some stage during the day.

As I lay there thinking about my future, clearly it was very uncertain, and my first task was to get through the operation. The surgeon came to see me and said that it would be in three stages – the priority was to get the tumour away from my spine and I presume it must have eroded some of the bones in that area because he said they would then have to put some form of scaffolding in place. After that they would attempt to remove the tumour entirely, but he thought it likely that they wouldn't be able to do that as it might be too much for me and he promised that at the first sign of danger they would pull out. Please forgive me if what I say isn't completely accurate, but that's the gist of what I can remember. Technically and medically it may well be wide of the mark. The truth is that I didn't really want to know all the detail, but I know that they have to tell you all the gruesome details because you have to sign the form to give permission for them to carry out the operation in these days of compensation culture, so it's only right that you know exactly what it is you're agreeing to, even if like me you'd rather be spared all the gory details!

The operation itself is a complete blank, as of course it should be, and I can't remember anything from being wheeled down to theatre and given the anaesthetic until coming round for some reason believing I was on the set of A Question Of Sport but looking from a balcony over New York's skyline at night! Just like any other dream really, not making any sense at all in the cold light of day but extremely vivid and logical at the time.

The long hours which followed the op were similarly vague, but the drugs I was being given were clearly giving me a number of false images and situations, and it wasn't long before my family started to doubt everything I said! Not much new in that scenario though, I might add!

I was fully aware that it was New Year's Day and that I'd had an operation, but I think almost everything else in my mind turned out to be fig-leaves of my imagination, however realistic it all seemed to me! So it transpired that the nurse who came into my room, said Good Morning to me before producing such a negative noise from her mouth which I interpreted as meaning that she'd had a late night celebrating the arrival of the New Year and was probably coming to work straight from the party, didn't exist at all! Days went by before I would accept this, as I clearly saw her have a quick wash at my sink before going out on the ward where I heard her telling one of her colleagues that she didn't feel very well, though she vehemently denied having over-imbibed during the previous few hours. I remember her being offered an injection to ease her pain, and her refusing it because she had a phobia about needles. She went into the room next to mine (I don't even know if there was a room next to mine!) for a lie down, and just before I dozed off I heard one of the other nurses say they were going to get her parents to come in and either persuade her to have the jab or take her home. When I woke up the next time she was still arguing, but this time her parents were involved too! I don't know what happened to her after that, but presumably she returned to the innermost recesses of my mind from where she had evidently come!

Once my visitors had started to find flaws in some of the stories I was relaying to them, they began to disbelieve everything I said, and I remember swearing blind that one of the nurses who'd washed me that morning was called Janine and came from Port Sunlight and they all laughed, presuming that I'd got confused and that it was probably the soap which had its origins in the Wirral and not the person using it! On that occasion, though, the nurse in question just happened to pass by and confirmed that that particular detail at least was correct!

The staff were all really good with me throughout my time in hospital, so my praise of them will be a recurring theme throughout this story, and by the time I left I had reason to be grateful to hundreds of different 'angels' to whom I shall always be indebted. The passage of time has now meant that I can no longer recall the names of the majority of them, but that in no way lessens the gratitude I felt and still feel towards nearly all of them, with only one or two exceptions. And it wasn't just the doctors, surgeons and nurses, either – there were physios, occupational therapists, a chiropodist or podiatrist as they seem to be called these days, radiographers, technicians, porters, admin staff, chaplains, volunteers and goodness knows who else, even a visiting artist and I mustn't omit to include a number of my fellow patients too! Let's put it this way – if it hadn't been for all these wonderful people, I wouldn't still be here now, considerably more than three years on…!

And while I'm giving out accolades, there's some more that I mustn't forget, as listed in my Dedication at the beginning of the book – top of the list is my immediate family, Su and the kids, though as they're now in their twenties perhaps I shouldn't refer to them as such! Then there's the other members of my close family – older brothers Bob and Alan and my twin sister Barbara and their families too. Su's sister Chris came up from Wales to help out when she could as well. And my friends, work colleagues, fellow football supporters, etc., all those who took the time and trouble to write and send all those get-well cards, letters and presents, send text messages, visit or just pray for my wellbeing. To say I was overwhelmed by the fantastic support I have received throughout this difficult time is the understatement to end all understatements. I found it very emotional to become aware how lucky I was to have the support of so many people, but it concerned me that this tearful state to which I became extremely prone might be misinterpreted as self-pity. Some of my condition was probably brought on by the drugs which I had to take, and at the time I was at a loss to explain why I had become so affected, because it really wasn't like me at all. I can only surmise that I was overwhelmed by the thought of all these members of my family and so many friends rooting for me! I found it quite upsetting to see the sad faces of people I cared about suffering because of me but it gave me an even greater incentive to come through the ordeal as best as I could. Not that I didn't have sufficient motivation anyway, but all the support that I received from what seemed like everyone I knew or had ever known brought home to me that feeling that I owed it to them as well as to myself to give it my best shot – so I did!

Chapter 2

Settling In!

The surgeon who had performed my op came to see me early in the New Year and said that all had gone as well as they had dared to hope. They'd moved the tumour away from my spine and put some sort of metal scaffolding in place to strengthen where it had been eroded, but then my physical condition meant they had to withdraw before completing the removal of the tumour, though it was anticipated that they would be able to treat what was left with radiotherapy. Forgive my amateurish attempts at relating the details of the operation, but the truth is that I never wanted to know all the minutiae of what had gone on, so as a result I'm not in a position to pass it on with any guarantee of accuracy. The important thing for me was to know that I was still in the land of the living, but would have to undergo further treatment to give me a reasonable chance of staying there for any length of time!

In the few days following my operation I had various other tests, partly to check on my progress, but also to try to determine the primary source of my cancer. On the 8th of January I was wheeled off for my initial visit to the radiotherapy department, ostensibly or so I thought for the first of what were likely to be six doses and I think it's something of an understatement to say that I wasn't looking forward to it at all! As it turned out, most of my fears were unfounded and as with everything else the nurses were superb with me. This first visit to the radiotherapy department wasn't part of the treatment at all but was actually like a survey to ensure that when I did go to have it done they would 'zap' me in the right place. It felt like I was being marked up for target practice, which in a sense I was, except that it wasn't for practice, it was for the real thing. I seem to remember a voice saying that it was T9 but at the time this didn't mean anything to me. I gather now that the area where they had put the metalwork in my back covered an area something like T8-T12 so, if that makes it sound like a game of Battleships, I suppose that in a way it was! Once they'd put the mark of Cain on me I was wheeled back to the ward, none the worse for the ordeal but more familiar with what to expect the next time I was taken there, which was the following day, presumably before anyone had the chance to wash off my target! These trips weren't straightforward procedures, I should tell you, because don't forget I wasn't able to move myself and everything had to be done with great care, otherwise someone might have had the even more unpleasant task of scraping me off the ceiling! They had to use a board to slide me from one surface to another, in this case from my bed to a hospital trolley, all very efficiently done, but it took three or four of them each time. They didn't take me straight there for my second visit, however, as the Occupational Therapy department had put in their request for the pleasure of my company. They wanted to measure me for a brace which it was hoped would help me to make progress with the physios by acting as a firm support for my back. That turned out to be something of an ordeal as they put this hot material on me which had to be moulded round my curvy contours and meant I had to remain motionless for quite a time. That would have been okay if the brace had done what it was supposed to do but unfortunately for me it didn't and despite all their efforts it never actually benefited me very much at all. I had quite a few trips down to their department as they made alterations to it but it never quite seemed right and though it followed me everywhere I went it was eventually discarded as ultimately I did what I was supposed to do without its help.

Once they had finished with me in OT that day my 'chauffeurs' took me on the second stage of my adventure. By this time Su and Chris had come to visit and were told on the ward that I had gone to radiotherapy, so they made their way there only to be told I hadn't arrived! Eventually I did get there but didn't have time to say more than "Hello" to them before I was whisked into the room where it was all going to happen – they slide you on to the table then bugger off so they don't get radiographied as well! But before they left me a new chap appeared out of the shadows as if from nowhere and said I wasn't going to need the six doses as I'd been told, one would be enough. He also told me that the illness I had got was myeloma, the first time that word had been mentioned to me! And with that he vanished, just as quickly as he'd arrived! Food for thought? You're not kidding! At first I thought it was good news, it surely can't be a bad thing to only need one treatment when you think you're going to have six. But then the doubts start to creep in – why am I only being given one when yesterday they told me I needed six? Perhaps I'm so far gone the other five would be wasted, and giving them to me would be pointless! I tried not to let that one stay in my mind long and I think I succeeded to a degree, and if I hadn't it would have been a wasted thought, wouldn't it, or surely I wouldn't still be here now, would I?

The actual radiotherapy for me was much ado about nothing, far less traumatic than I'd dreaded it might be. I'm sure it is very painful for many people, and since those days I've had first-hand confirmation that it is, so maybe I was just one of the lucky few, but I can at least bear testament that it isn't necessarily going to be as painful or tortuous as one might anticipate, and I was back on the ward almost before I knew it, and none the worse for the experience! I was introduced to Clare and Stuart for the first time and told that they were haematology nurses who specialised in looking after patients with the sort of cancer I had got, and they would be our contacts should we need any help or information. One morning soon after Stuart called to see me and said that he needed to carry out a procedure on me as part of their investigations, presumably to confirm that the myeloma diagnosis was the correct one. This was a biopsy and would involve him sticking a needle into my bone somewhere round my hip in order to extract some bone marrow to test, I think. More of my amateurish description here, I'm afraid, but I feel queasy just writing about it now so you can imagine how I must have felt back then! I think that's what he said anyway and he needed me to agree to it and sign a form before he could proceed. I asked him when he was planning to do it and he said "in about five minutes!" Not much time to get too worked up about it then, but long enough for me to ring Su to let her know what was going on. I have to say that both Stuart and Clare have been brilliant from that first time I met them, with Su as well as with me, and Stuart guided me through this ordeal superbly. He talked quietly about what he was doing as he did it and what I could expect to feel at each stage, and before I knew it it was all done and dusted and he'd got his evidence. It wasn't long before the results were available and Stuart and Clare came to tell me along with Dr.Kanyike, who was to be my specialist doctor. They confirmed that it was indeed multiple myeloma, cancer of the bone marrow, and although it wasn't curable, it was at least treatable with chemotherapy. I had hardly ever heard of myeloma before and the only person whom I can associate with it is Jack Rosenthal, the well-known playwright and television writer who died from it in 2004 and it is his widow, actress Maureen Lipman, whose face adorns posters for the charity Myeloma UK. You will undoubtedly understand if I tell you that this is one of the causes which I am hoping we'll be able to support with any proceeds we happen to make from this book.

The chemotherapy which they were proposing to start at the end of January would be in tablet form, which sounded a lot better to my ears than what I'd envisaged might be the case. It was called CTD, each of those letters being the initial letter of one of the tablets I would have to take. For the technically-minded among you who like to know these things, these were Cyclophosphamide, Thalidomide and Dexamethasone, and all those of you of a certain age, like me, will doubtless be familiar with that middle one. Well it may have had a bad press way back in the sixties, but it seems to have done alright by me! I was given a timetable showing which tablet had to be taken when, and how many of each. There would be six cycles of three weeks each, and each cycle would be separated by a week off. I would have to take different quantities of each of the tablets, for instance I had to have Thalidomide every day of the three weeks but one of the others only had to be taken one day a week while the third one had so many days on and so many off. You are so engrossed with it at the time that you'd think you would never forget all the little details, but of course with the passage of time (and the onset of old age!) you do! I can't remember the ins and outs of it now but back then even though it was a little bit complicated to start with we soon got used to it. We were given a booklet which outlined what the treatment entailed and listed the possible side-effects. There seemed to be so many that you'd think you would be bound to suffer some of them, but it left you wondering if they just list everything so that you can't turn round later and say you hadn't been warned! And some seemed to contradict themselves, like putting constipation and diarrhoea as possibles for the same drug! In the event I didn't do too badly regarding these side-effects and the only one I can recall, and Clare said it was possible that this would never completely disappear, was a condition called peripheral neuropathy. I must have only had this at a low level because I believe it can be quite serious whereas for me it only meant that the outside of my right hand from my little finger down to my wrist is inclined to be quite numb, there's hardly any feeling in it. It's a bit strange, but compared to some of the other side-effects I saw it's not too bad at all. The booklet also had space in for me to list anything I might consider relevant and there was a printed timetable too to make sure we knew what tablets had to be taken and when. Suffice to say that at the peak of my treatment I was starting off some days by taking 35 pills at one go! This isn't quite as bad as it sounds as most of them were very small and I was able to take them five at a time. It was hoped that once I'd done the full six cycles the treatment would be complete, and then it was fingers and everything else crossed after that that just maybe the cancer would go into remission for as long as possible.

By this time I had been back on Ward 17 for a couple of weeks, that being where I had been admitted originally Once the crucial first few days after my op had been safely negotiated, it was felt I could safely be moved out of Ward 2 where almost everything is done for you and back to Ward 17. I still needed most things doing for me, but gradually I would start to manage odd bits for myself. That was inevitably going to take time, though, so in the meantime I had to get used to the daily routines which probably don't vary much whichever hospital you are in.

The lights would be switched on at some ungodly hour like six o'clock for a cup of tea, and those who were capable would be encouraged to get up and carry out their morning ablutions. That didn't include me, for the simple reason that I could neither get out of bed nor wash myself. I soon did manage to start washing my hands and face and as far as I could reach on my front, but I couldn't reach my nether regions or my back, legs or feet. so they had to wait till later in the morning.

Back in the days when I was working for a living, a recurring theme in conversations between me and one of my workmates, Bob, was how we thought we might cope if we were ever faced with a situation such as I was now finding myself in, involving having to have everything done for you. We were both in total agreement that it would be quite impossible, we wouldn't be able to face it and would probably die, at the very least of embarrassment! Yet here I was, happily submitting to every little procedure, however personal, intimate or intrusive it might be. I couldn't really believe it myself, but when faced with the alternative I didn't have any choice. Once you become fully aware that the nurses don't mind at all and just take it in their stride as part of their job, and you know there's no way round it, it doesn't take long for you to accept whatever is being done to you. I had been catheterised within hours of my arrival in hospital so that was rather a rude awakening to start off with

(I was used to people taking the piss out of me metaphorically, but this was the first time it had happened to me literally!), and after that everything seemed to just be taken for granted. Even suppositories and enemas became the order of the day for a while! And neither Su nor I will ever forget the day I rang her up to ask her to guess where I was – I was suspended from a hoist with my head near the ceiling and my rear end lined up over a bedpan! Well, you either laughed or cried and dignity was the prerogative of other people while I was in there, and certainly not for me! It was clearly no big deal for them and there were many more in the same boat as I was so it was just easier to accept it and get on with it.

Breakfast arrived about 8-ish, a choice of cereals or porridge, and some were allowed a cooked breakfast, as approved by a dietician. I eventually became included in this elite band, but it turned out not to be quite as appetising as it sounded to my hungry ears. They couldn't offer any eggs except scrambled (and even that was mass-produced more than likely from a powdered version – yuk!), and any bacon on offer was the cheapest cut you could hope not to find! So while it was a novelty to get something labelled a 'cooked breakfast', it turned out to be quite a let-down, I'm sorry to say.

Sadly too, this was my overall impression of the food throughout my latter time in hospital, to the extent that I was hardly eating anything in my last few weeks there. But it had been so different in my earlier days… It seemed quite a novelty to be given quite a wide range of choices for lunch and dinner, and in the first few weeks after my op I seemed to develop a much greater appetite than had been my norm for months. I happily chose from the menus, even though we had to mark up our choices a day in advance, and I ate everything that was put in front of me. I even managed to eat some chocolate-covered prunes which Alison, our Christopher's other half, brought in specially, and that wasn't something I would ever have considered normally. After a couple of months, though, the repetitive nature of the fare on offer led to me becoming quite disenchanted with it and I started to become quite critical of it as a result. Even the meat on the sandwiches was rubbery (to which a Chinaman might say, "Ah, I'm grad you rike it!" – sorry!!!) so my normal standby had little to attract me. The exception was the selection of soups which became my main source of sustenance in the last couple of months I was there. Oh yes, not forgetting the cornflakes in the morning too – where would I have been without them?!

A lot of this negativity was my own fault really – I've always been a fussy eater ("faddy" my mother used to call it!), but it was more of a surprise that I ate so well early on than was my limited eating later. I couldn't even work up any interest in taking up my visitors' many offers to bring things in for me, though I did manage to 'force down' the pies which Bob, Kath & Lynn, friends from work, brought for me one night, knowing my weakness for this particular bakery's products! Overall my lack of appetite at certain times was probably simply because I was, after all, still not well!

Once breakfast was out of the way we were more often than not left to our own devices. For me that usually meant sleep, as I never showed much interest in doing anything else apart from reading a daily paper which we could buy from "Mr.Squeakie" as the man from the newsagents who wheeled his trolley round the wards came to be known due to his high-pitched call announcing his wares.

The nurses obviously had all their routine jobs to do, making beds and the like, and they would normally fit this around the time that the patient was in the bathroom. My inability to even sit up without support meant this was impossible and they had to do it round me, moving me first one way, then the other. It was a little uncomfortable for me, but their skill at adapting the procedure meant it wasn't too bad.

Medical routines were prominent too, of course. The ward round in the morning featured your specialist with members of his team just checking everything was progressing as it should, often accompanied by students learning their trade. Then every few hours you could be sure one of the nurses would come round doing your "obs" – a threefold procedure involving taking your temperature, blood pressure and pulse rate. I had a tendency to have a high temperature first thing in the morning, but a couple of paracetamols usually ensured that it was back to normal by lunchtime. And there would usually be a visit from one of the ward doctors at some stage most days, just as a routine generally, but these visits were more regular if they were concerned about any symptoms you might be displaying.

The dispensing of medicines and pills was another regular routine which took place about four times a day and which on occasions was more than welcome, depending on the level of pain or discomfort you were suffering at the time, and that brings me to another regular test which had to be endured rather than enjoyed – the blood test!

My lifelong phobia where needles are concerned has been one of the more difficult aspects of my illness (I used to call it prickophobia but I think that sometimes got misinterpreted!), but I've had so many jabs and tests since first entering hospital that I almost take them in my stride nowadays. I'd rather not have to have them but at least I don't feel that I'm going to keel over in a dead faint every time someone approaches me with a needle. This is just as well because I still have to have one in my stomach every night, and this one Su very kindly does for me as I doubt that my tolerance of them could ever stretch as far as my being able to administer them to myself.

As I've already said, most of the time you are in hospital you are free to occupy yourself as you think fit and it's up to you how you spend your time, so long as someone official knows where you are and you are available for any tests or procedures when needed. I was obviously very limited in what was open to me, being bed-ridden all the time I was in hospital. This is where you become the captive audience for the 'scam' known as Patientline! The idea is wonderful, but if you use it as they hope you will you'll soon find that you are extremely disadvantaged financially as a result! It has two aspects to it, the phone and the television/radio. Fortunately, there has been a relaxing of the rule in hospitals which used to ban the use of mobile phones, and that has eased the burden of one side of Patientline. Prior to that anyone trying to contact you directly by phone might need to take out a second mortgage to afford the cost of ringing you directly. Yes, it sounds really good that you are allocated your own phone number when admitted to hospital, but it really should come complete with a government health warning advising you how much it may be about to cost you or any of your unsuspecting well-wishers! However, in reality nearly all patients will be reassured to know that mobile phones are now not only permitted, you are also allowed to charge them up on the wards – or you can if you are able to find an available socket, and it must be said that this is far easier said than done sometimes!

As far as the television side of Patientline was concerned, they'd got you by the proverbial "s & c's" – it was a case of pay-up or do without! What really rankled was that I was already paying the best part of £100 a month for the 'works' at home – over 100 channels (even though a high percentage never got watched because they're crap!) including the sports and the films + the Virginmedia box + phone rental and calls + broadband internet, yet now I was being asked to fork out another tenner every few days in order to choose from a much smaller selection of channels. The principle was very good, at least I was able to watch something, but what they charged for the service was bordering on extortionate!

It's surprising looking back how little I did bearing in mind that I was in hospital for five months. I didn't have the physical ability to move many parts of my body, which is a bit limiting to start off with! I couldn't even turn over or sit up without assistance, so it's hardly surprising that thinking, praying and sleeping became the most common activities into which I channelled my efforts. It's not uncommon for even a non-religious person to call on Divine help in times of great adversity, so it's hardly surprising that I, having had the strong Catholic upbringing that I had, would return to my traditional sources for support and strength. Word got round and I was given Holy Communion from time to time during my hospitalisation and later as well after I had been transferred to Cuerden Grange.

I suspect that many people who have had lengthy stays in hospital would probably say that they found it quite boring and I suppose it's true to a large extent. For the most part you are expected to make your own entertainment if you want any. I doubt that we'll ever find hospital variety shows funded by the NHS. Also, as everything in there is dependent on routine, all days tend to be the same or very similar. Accordingly, if anything happens which is only slightly out of the ordinary, it tends to get flagged up as a highlight. At the lower end of the scale is the sudden demise of a patient. I know this happened more than once during my stay in Royal Preston but I was relieved to know it didn't occur close by or to anyone I had got to know. The signs were pretty obvious, though, as without warning all the curtains were drawn round every bed until I presume the body in question had been removed and taken to the mortuary. At times like that you had to be philosophical and perhaps just a little grateful that at least it wasn't you!

I've mentioned earlier that I was catheterised soon after my arrival at hospital and this remained the case for much of my time as a patient. While this was far from ideal it solved certain obvious problems even if it did create the occasional other one. For anyone unfamiliar with the procedure the catheter is inserted into the appropriate part of one's anatomy while the other end (of the catheter, NOT the body!) is attached to a pipe which leads to a bag which hangs on the side of the bed. There is a tap on the bag so it can be drained easily but it does rely on someone being aware that it is due to be emptied. There were times when this didn't happen when it should have and this could potentially lead to further problems. One such was the teatime when mine sprung a leak! I don't know whether this was a fault on the bag itself or if the tap hadn't been properly turned off previously, but whatever the reason a river appeared to be flowing down the ward and it wouldn't have taken even the simplest explorer more than a few seconds to determine its source! But there is a golden rule in hospitals and, as I discovered later, in nursing homes too which says that toileting problems cannot be resolved at meal times. This is obviously to do with hygiene and I appreciate that no-one would want a member of staff to be serving food while at the same time sorting out a patient's toileting arrangements. However, it wasn't always convenient for the patient either and this became one occasion when it was the meal which had to be delayed.

I can never think about that particular incident without calling to mind something which we used to do in our teens, making up book or song titles where the author/singer would be an appropriate match for the title. Examples which spring to mind are "I Fell Out Of The Window" by Eileen Dover, "Natural History" by Teresa Green, "How To Succeed At Anything" by Percy Verance, "The Castrated Russian" by Ivor Bolokov, "Snooker Behind The Iron Curtain" by Inov The Red and the suitable one for this scenario, "The Yellow River" by I.P.Daly!

As my condition generally started to improve and I was becoming more aware of everything around me, Su felt the time was right to broach with me the subject of my appearance. I've never been one for spending much time looking at myself in a mirror, and the briefest of glances at any of the photos of me in this book will undoubtedly help you to understand why, but having been long overdue my customary visit to the barber's, 'scruffy' would not have been an inaccurate adjective to describe how I must have looked to anyone unfortunate enough to cast their eyes in my general direction.

As an inherently lazy person, I had realised more than thirty years ago that I didn't like shaving, and not only did I consider it a pain to have to undergo this ritual every day, I also reasoned that the time I spent doing it would be far better employed staying in bed for an extra few minutes. So I decided to grow a beard which also served the purpose of covering up some of my facial features. Nothing which has happened in the ensuing thirty-five years has ever made me think that that decision was a wrong one. It's perfectly honest as far as I'm concerned – it shouts out, "I Don't Like Shaving!" not "Don't I Look So Much Better With A Beard?"! I've no time for men who grow beards but shave part of their faces to 'style' them – that to me suggests that they really do think they are more attractive with facial hair. One consequence of my lack of shaving which has caused some amusement to me was the day I realised a few years ago that once Christopher left home for university, despite me being the only male left living in our house, I was actually the only inhabitant who didn't possess a razor!

Time hasn't been over-kind to me regarding the hair on top of my head, either. I've always claimed it was the kids who caused me to lose it but I think my once-wavy hair had started to wave bye-bye long before their arrival! My very high forehead, or baldness as it is more commonly known, has in the long term been another plus as far as I am concerned because it means that like my beard it doesn't require much attention. I do wash it, though, (at least twice a year whether it needs it or not!) and get my local barber to give both head and beard a 'number 1' so as not to look a complete tramp for any longer than necessary.

However, having been in hospital a few weeks, and having been admitted at a time when the aforementioned 'number 1' was due, hobo status was certainly coming my way by the end of January and Su decided it was time to do something about it at the earliest possible opportunity. So, no sooner had I started to spend a little bit of time in my newly-acquired wheelchair than she started turning her thoughts to how we could resolve my unkempt condition so that she could have her husband back, the phrase which she usually expresses whenever I've made my customary visit to the barber. There was a hairdresser's actually in the hospital close to the main entrance and we decided to give them a visit. We'd spent one visiting session out of the ward as a trial run so that I could get accustomed to being pushed in the wheelchair. Su made enquiries with the hairdresser and on February 9th I was taken on my first 'excursion' to restore my handsome visage to its former glory – insofar as there was any glory for it to be returned to! I can't deny that I did feel much better when it had been done and it was a significant step for me on the road back to normality. The nurses didn't recognise me when I got back to the ward and their comments were generally speaking quite positive, which may give you some notion as to how bad I must have looked beforehand.

I was very fortunate, unlike a number of my fellow patients, in that I was never short of visitors. Family, friends, some travelling long distances to call and see me, it was so gratifying to be made aware how concerned so many people had been while I was ill, and to note the lengths that some of them would go to in order to offer whatever support they could. I feel I should give special mention here to Debbie, Kath and Helen, my Skem ladies, because they have visited me wherever I have been – in hospital, at the nursing home and have also been to see me since I came back home, and these are ladies with whom I haven't worked directly since 1994! I can only presume that it must be my animal magnetism which keeps them coming to see me…!

Depending on which ward I was in, visiting times varied, but the usual was a couple of hours in the afternoon and the same again in the evening, usually finishing about 8 o'clock. Su came to see me every day, and more often than not she was with me for both sessions, going for a cuppa and maybe a bite to eat or perhaps a look round the local shops in between the two periods. The children visited most days too, especially in the early stages, and the rest of the family took turns to call as well. Add occasional visits from friends, former workmates, fellow football supporters etc. and you can see that I was never short of company. I felt quite guilty on many occasions when I was the only one in my 'bay' to be receiving visitors. Their continual presence certainly benefited me enormously through some of the darker days.

For someone who is normally regarded as something of an extrovert, a transformation seems to take place as soon as I enter a hospital. I retreat into myself and don't speak unless absolutely necessary. I am barely recognisable as the quite social animal who exists outside. However, once I'd been in hospital a little while this time I became more able to socialise, at least with my visitors. The last thing I wanted, though, was any in-depth discussion about my or anyone else's medical condition. Bad enough that I had to be in there, just do what you have to do and leave me alone otherwise. What a miserable bugger you must think I am!

As time went on, though, I tended to deal with situations a bit better. Some of the other patients were very good to me. They could see I wasn't able to get out of bed so they would offer to get my newspaper for me, or any sweets or bits from the hospital shop, or plug my phone into the charger, etc.. As a result I did become quite friendly with one or two other patients and was very grateful for what they did for me.

I'll have more to say about these lovely people in the next chapter, but before that I can't ignore that at the other end of the scale were one or two whose behaviour, I felt, left them wide open for the criticism I'm about to send in their direction. Yes, they were ill, but so were the rest of us, but we didn't all go on making a song-and-dance about it as some of them seemed to do! The trouble was, though, that as ever it was the ones who made all the noise who ended up getting preferential treatment. Don't get me wrong, I don't have a single negative word to say about the way I was treated in hospital, the nurses were absolutely brilliant, and all the other staff carried out their duties exactly as you would hope and expect in that situation. But their jobs are not made any easier by those who for some reason think they deserve better than everyone else, and NOW, not being prepared to wait till it's their turn. I suppose it would be more appropriate to call them 'impatients'. Thankfully they were few and far between and at least it gave the rest of us something to 'chunner' about other than muttering about our illnesses!

One such 'impatient' was Farooq (not his real name!), an Asian bloke who was probably in his mid-thirties. I know he had been very ill during his time in hospital and I always got the impression that most of the nurses seemed to have a soft spot for him, probably because after having had such a hard time he was by the time he appeared on our ward showing definite signs of improvement. However, in my view, and I know this was shared by all the other patients who were within hearing distance of him, the severity of his condition in no way entitled him to behave in the way that he did towards both the staff and his fellow patients.

Before I go any further let me stress that any criticism I had of Farooq had absolutely nothing to do with the colour of his skin or his culture and religious beliefs. It is purely governed by the way he treated all around him – the staff, fellow-patients and even visitors! My reaction to him would have been exactly the same if he had been a white man trying to impose himself and his beliefs on anyone within shouting distance of him. And believe me, forty-three years of dealing with members of the public has given me plenty of experience of seeing the negative side of human nature.

Initially Farooq seemed very harmless, if a little eccentric. He interrogated every patient who was prepared to accommodate his mode of questioning. He would seek details of patients' illnesses and treatments and offer advice to each. Then, standing in the middle of the ward with his arms aloft he would announce that he would pray for them, which he did – and loudly! If I sensed he was coming in my direction I would pretend to be asleep and he either took the hint or was duped by my cunning ways!

Not a lot to complain about so far, I hear you say! Agreed! But unfortunately it didn't stop there. He started to scrounge food and sweets from anyone prepared to take him on, and would also either ask people to wheel him to the hospital shop or go there on his behalf. Bear in mind that this is a big hospital and the ward was on the third floor, whereas the shop was on the ground floor near the entrance, so it meant it was quite a trek for any poor unsuspecting souls. They felt obliged to help, so he hardly ever got a refusal. He even collared my sister Barbara one night, intercepting her as she was on her way to see me. As she said to me later, she didn't feel she could say no. He gave my son a letter to post on his way out on another occasion, and the next time he saw him asked if he had indeed posted it. Christopher said he felt like telling him that as soon as he'd left he'd thrown it in the bin, which of course he hadn't!

Then there was the incessant chanting – for hours in the night, and if it wasn't that in his own language it was his life story in broken English repeated endlessly over and over again. "FAROOQ, WILL YOU SHUT THE F**K UP!!" I used to shout at the top of my voice, but only in my head!! Eventually I did pluck up courage to ask him to tone it down one afternoon when there were only the two of us in the ward, and for a while he did. Mind you, it wasn't long before I heard him chunnering about it being a free country and he wasn't doing any harm, etc. etc.

And why was he the only one in the ward who played his radio loud enough for everyone else to hear? As luck would have it, his choice of music wasn't so bad, but he had no right, as none of us had, to determine what everyone else had to listen to. Isn't that why they issue you with headphones, to ensure you don't disturb anyone else?

Well, seeing as I'm having a proper whinge about him, I might as well not hold anything back! When he used his phone, it was almost as if he didn't need it, I think he could have made himself heard without the instrument. And it always seemed to be his bank he was ringing, so he could share his financial problems with everyone else. God (or Allah!) help the poor person at the other end of the line! He didn't appear to have grasped that basic principle that if you haven't got any money in the bank you can't really expect them to let you take any out!

You are probably aware that every bed is equipped with a buzzer for patients to press to summon nursing staff when they need something. This is only really intended for emergencies and most people would limit their use of this facility to essentials, but not Farooq. The slightest whim and 'buzz'! And woe betide if they kept him waiting, he would then scream at the top of his voice so that it became obvious that a dire emergency was taking place. Imagine the response when the nurse arrived to be told that he needed a spoon so that he could eat his yoghurt!

By the time he left the hospital everyone in the ward knew his full life story because he repeated it (to himself, supposedly, but always out loud) day after day after day. It was indeed a joyful time for all, no doubt for him too, when everything was put in place to enable him to go home. I wasn't convinced that he was well enough or capable to manage on his own, but I cannot deny that it felt like a whole weight had been lifted from the ward when he went. I don't think I could have tolerated his presence there for much longer and would probably have gone 'round the bend' if he hadn't been discharged when he was. I do hope for everyone's sake, not least his own, that his recovery has continued and that he has found some level of happiness which clearly seemed to have eluded him up until then.

Chapter 3

Patients

It has to be said that Farooq was very much the exception amongst all the patients with whom I had any contact while I was in hospital. As I just mentioned, I have spent most of my adult life dealing with the great British public, and it has long been my opinion that the vast majority are basically okay. There may only be a small percentage with whom you become quite friendly, but most of the rest are still fine. Sad to say, though, at the other end of the scale there are always that tell-tale few who rub you up the wrong way. Dealings with them inevitably ruin your day, and spoil any positives you may have accrued during all the rest of the day. Well it's no different in hospital, and why would it not be? You're dealing with a cross-section of Joe Public just the same, with the one possibly only thing you have definitely got in common being that you are all sick! So it can't be surprising that the odd one, and in some cases really odd ones (!), may not exactly be your cup of tea!

I came across some wonderful characters while I was in the various wards in Royal Preston. Like the old chap who wondered why he couldn't see through his glasses properly, then I overheard him telling his visitors that he'd bought them at a car boot sale! And another old fella who had received a get-well card from his local football team, and it had been signed by everyone, or so it seemed, from the chairman and manager, through many of the players, right down to the tea-lady. And if I told you that the side in question was Accrington Stanley, you may well ask "Who?" and I would have to reply "Exactly!" If you don't remember that milk commercial from years ago with the Ian Rush reference, that last exchange will have been completely lost on you, but never mind. The truth of the matter though is that I knew all about Accrington Stanley as my local non-league team (Chorley) had spent many seasons in the same leagues as them, but in recent years they have left us far behind and while my team languishes still in the lower reaches of non-league, they are enjoying the comparative heady heights of Division Two of the Football League, and have only just missed out on promotion to Division One. Still, I couldn't begrudge him the pleasure that this gesture had obviously given him, but it did start to wear a bit thin when we got into the fourth day and he was still showing it to every one who set foot in our bay, not only those who were visiting him but everyone else's visitors too, and any unsuspecting member of staff, and every time with the same commentary..!

I too was on the receiving end of a kind gesture initiated by a fellow Chorley supporter, Darren Fishwick, and he went to the trouble of printing a poster on which were the words "Chorley FC Missing Mr.JB". He took this to a game and persuaded other supporters and the management team at the time to have their photos taken holding it. I then received through the post a set of the resultant photographs which had the desired effect of perking me up noticeably. Unfortunately the manager at the time left the club soon after to take over at Lancaster, a club in the same league as us, and I only mention this because as a curious coincidence the chap who did the announcements over the loudspeakers at Lancaster was also in the same ward as I was for a couple of weeks – small world, eh? Having said that, we didn't fall out over it, possibly because it didn't happen till after he was discharged!

If ever I started to feel sorry for myself while I was in hospital there was always something to help me put my situation into perspective. If it wasn't seeing world events on TV where people were losing their livelihoods and in many cases even their lives through wars or natural disasters, then I only needed to look around me and see some of the younger lads who had been struck down by cancer, and marvel at how upbeat most of them were and how well they seemed to cope with it. I very much doubt that I would have been able to do so had I been faced with it at that time of my life.

I do wonder from time to time how some of my fellow-patients are getting on now, especially the younger ones. Also people like Andrew, my saviour so often during the Farooq days. He was in the next bed to mine and all that stood, or to be more accurate lay, between me and the aforementioned source of our grievances. We got all our mutterings about him off our chests when he wasn't around, and if we hadn't done that then it's just possible one or both of us might have got into trouble for telling him exactly what we thought. Despite all I've written here, I genuinely didn't wish Farooq any ill and as I said at the end of the last chapter I sincerely hope he was able to recover physically and perhaps find some contentment in his life.

I really felt sorry for Andrew – he was obviously a good sort and when I first met him he had already been in hospital for five months, and it appeared that they had still not managed to get to the bottom of what was actually the matter with him. He'd had a couple of spells in Intensive Care with pneumonia but by the time I met him he had managed to get mobile to a degree, albeit only in a wheelchair. At least that meant he was able to get out to the car park occasionally for a smoke. I'm thankful I had managed to kick that particular habit some years before all this took place as my immobility would have meant it would have been impossible for me to indulge at all. Having said that, I am known to like the odd alcoholic beverage myself (and a few even ones as well!), and I never had a single one (or any doubles for that matter!) all the time I was in hospital, and I can honestly say that I never missed it at all, though you wouldn't have guessed if you saw the speed at which I sought to make up for it once I was out of hospital!

Andrew's new mobility meant that he was able to go on home visits at weekend to Burnley, and you could tell how much that meant to him. Understandable of course, but that was something I couldn't possibly aspire to, not while I was in hospital at any rate, nor for a few months after. When I last saw Andrew he was still in limbo, bored to the point of distraction, on the list waiting to go to a specialised spinal unit, but in the meantime stuck in hospital, with all its limitations.

Then there was Tony on Ribblesdale Ward. Whereas Andrew was probably only in his forties or early fifties, Tony was possibly even older than yours truly. I know he and his wife celebrated their Ruby Wedding while he was stuck in hospital, so they were a few years ahead of Su and me in that regard. His home was only about a mile from ours and just across the road from one of the nursing homes we considered I might move to when I left hospital. Tony soon became aware of my limitations and made a point of helping me out in whatever way he could. Usually this meant getting my morning paper for me but he also offered me the use of any reading matter he had and was always on hand to get anything for me which was out of my reach. I missed him when he was discharged, though I was obviously pleased for him, but I needn't have worried because it wasn't long before others took over where he left off, and I had cause to be grateful to a number of them during my long period of incapacity.

Unfortunately it wasn't long before Tony was readmitted, and he really wasn't well at all. Su came across him in a side room one afternoon on her way to visit me as he called to her as she was passing and he was most anxious to know how I was progressing. I never saw him again after that and have since heard that he has passed away – very sad, but inevitable that some patients won't survive their stay in hospital. It just makes you even more aware how lucky you are if you do manage to get back home for some kind of normal existence.

The Blackburn family! Bob &Alan at the back, the twins at the front on their 60th birthday

Darren Fishwick with Christopher and the goodwill message!

With Ian on the steps of Toddington Manor in the Cotswolds in 2008

Presenting the Jack Kirkland Trophy to P.N.E.'s Chris Brown

Chapter 4

Crisis!

By this time, even though we were barely out of January it seemed as if I'd been in hospital for ever. In myself I wasn't feeling too bad, all things considered, and I vaguely wondered when I might be able to go home. The medical team who had performed my operation had declared there was nothing more for them to do, it had gone as well as they dared to hope it would and I'd had radiotherapy as well to 'zap' what was left of the tumour. The physios had done what they could to try to get me back on my feet but that hadn't gone according to plan. It took three of them to get me to a sitting position and that was painful enough, but when they tried to stand me up on my feet I was all over the place, figuratively if not literally. I was dizzy and felt faint, my blood pressure went haywire and eventually they had to concede defeat. They said they wouldn't abandon me altogether but they would set their sights somewhat lower, like just helping me with some basic exercises which I could do while lying in bed. On reflection it was a pity we didn't persevere but I really couldn't do much and it seemed like I was just wasting time that they could spend more profitably with someone else. I bet they'd be amazed if they could see the progress I have made since as there was nothing at the time to suggest I would ever be able to stand on my own two feet again, let alone actually walk. They were a lovely group of girls and as with many of the nurses it's a shame I've forgotten nearly all their names, all except for Amy who was in charge of the team and I couldn't ever forget Kelly from Coppull! She was very much a beginner and just learning the job, but she was lovely and I was really sorry when she said she had done her few weeks in that department and was having to move on.

Before they left me to my own devices they gave me a few basic exercises to try to do when I could, not much more than raising my legs from the bed, a far harder proposition at that stage than you might think. They had done some bending of my joints – knees and feet, and they thought Su might be able to do some of those with me. They also introduced us to the practice of toe-towelling, as its name suggests a kind of massaging of the toes using a towel! Su did quite a lot of that over the next few weeks, as well as regularly putting E45 cream on my feet, a practice which reminded me of Roman emperors lying back while their servants/slaves did everything for them! "Ee, lass, crush me a grape!" Not that I ever said that out loud to her, though! As it isn't the type of activity I could ever have asked anyone else to do for me, I must mention one of my special friends from work in this context, Nikki, as she actually volunteered to do that for me one day. That's when it brought home to me how special she is, but at the risk of repeating myself yet again the main positive to have come out of everything that has happened to me over the last few years has been the realisation that I am surrounded by a wonderful family and a very special group of friends.

This lack of progress was clearly not going to help in my quest to get back home, even though that's what everyone wanted. Our house was totally unsuitable to accommodate a disabled patient which was clearly what I was. My situation at that time meant that we would definitely have to have an extension built to accommodate me or at the very least have some radical alterations done to the inside of the house. We soon learned that we would have to bear all the expense of any alterations which were made. The lump sum which I received as a result of my decision to retire meant that any means test we had would inevitably go against us, but that became something we would just have to accept. Maybe I wouldn't have handed my notice in when I did had I known this was waiting for me round the corner, but it was too late to do anything about that now. To dwell on it would have made us very bitter, and worse would come a few months later when we learned that I would have to be transferred to a nursing home at a cost of more than £500 per week. So we took a deep breath – then stumped up whatever money was required!

By this time Su was starting to have health problems of her own. She had had one of her hips replaced a few years earlier and we knew that one day she would have to have the other one done as well. It soon became apparent that that time was fast approaching. She struggled on for a few months but was clearly not in any fit state to act as a carer for a disabled husband.

We reached a kind of stalemate after a while. The hospital said they couldn't do much more for me as the chemotherapy I was having could be self-administered at home, and inevitably they wanted the bed to accommodate someone else. I couldn't go home because neither the house nor Su were in a position to receive me. However, before anything could be decided, fate stepped in and forced its own hand...

On February 13th I had been transferred to Ribblesdale Ward, which specialises in looking after cancer patients. At first I had been reluctant to go there as I was being well looked after where I was in Ward 17 and had got to know and like the staff there. It didn't take me long to settle in on Ribblesdale, though, and soon it was as if I'd never been anywhere else. What was unusual and took a bit of getting used to was the incessant beeping of myriad machines in the ward. There was always at least one person within earshot who was on chemotherapy and/or attached to a machine programmed to beep when a process was complete or make a different noise if there was a problem with the procedure. Sometimes this could grate a bit but in time I grew accustomed to it and of course on occasions the machines in question were attached to me!

While I continue to say that I was well cared for wherever I went, I must make special mention here of a few of the nurses on Ribblesdale Ward who were especially good to me. Lisa always seemed to be the one who was there when I was feeling particularly low, and nothing was ever too much trouble for her. She even came to visit me when I was on other wards, and has kept in touch since I left hospital. I called her Lisa T to distinguish her from a number of other Lisas in my circle of friends but she recently asked me why I called her that when her surname begins with H! Between you, me and the gatepost I think she's forgotten her name or changed it to escape from her past, because it can't possibly be that I've made a mistake or misheard her name – can it?! Anyway it's too late for me to change it now as I've already got a Lisa H in my list of contacts so I've told her she'll have to marry someone with a surname beginning with a T or change her name by deed poll!

Then there was Chris, one of the few male nurses who looked after me – we used to wind each other up in a way that is not always wise to do when dealing with members of the opposite sex, not if you want to remain attached to your family jewels anyway! And I was extremely vulnerable in that department too so discretion was certainly the better part of valour as I confined my insults to Chris – his back was broad enough and he could give as good as he received too!

Carol was a Chorley girl and you could tell as soon as she opened her mouth! If that sounds like a negative, it isn't meant to be – I was born and brought up there, so we had something of an affinity from the word 'go'. Just ask us to say 'bus' and when it comes out with a double z you won't be surprised at where we come from! When my beard reached that stage again when if I could have stood up I might have tripped up over it, it was Carol who came to my rescue by bringing in appropriate implements from home and giving it a tidy trim! In return I listened to her complaints about her family and thoughtless people who insisted on parking outside her house despite the fact that they had a permit allowing only them to park there. That more or less made us quits!

Another Chorley lass who was very good to me in there was Sandra, a bit older than most of the others and more senior in rank as well. When not working at the hospital she ran her own bakery though she never let me sample any of the goodies from there. Mind you, what she failed to give me to put in my mouth she more than made up for by either giving me enemas at the other end of my anatomy or by delegating other of her colleagues to do so!

Michelle was the practical joker on that ward and I think it's fair to say that we didn't exactly get off on the right foot. She had spotted the newspapers on my table and came over to have a read, but I thought she was intending to throw them away and was about to stop her till I realised that unlike one or two of the others she was happy for me to let them pile up if that was what I wanted. And it was Michelle who bought me a bacon butty from their canteen and paid for it out of her own pocket when she saw how keen I was to have one, as it wasn't an item to be found on the ordinary patients' menu. I still think, though, that she was a bit cruel telling another of the nurses, who clearly came from the far east (China, not Middlesbrough!), that she would have to register a new patient coming in who was Scottish and his name was Angus McCoatup!

And to prove I'm not racist, there were a couple of Scousers on the ward who were always good for a laugh too, Maggs and her mate Tina. I'm not noted for having imparted much in the way of education to many people over the years, but I know that Maggs still remembers the day I taught her the word 'pedantic'. Being classed as a pedant myself, especially where the use and abuse of apostrophe's (Grrr! It hurts even to write it like that by way of illustration!) are concerned, it wasn't difficult for me to interpret that her husband held similar views to mine, but I just told her to tell him, when he was laying down his principles to her, not to be so pedantic! Unfortunately she had forgotten what the word was by the time she got home so we had to go over it all again the next day! I saw her one day last year after one of my checkups, though, and she still remembered me for that if for nothing else!

I continued to make progress while on Ribblesdale, even if it was slow and barely noticeable, nonetheless we all felt that at least there were some steps in the right direction. The length of time I was able to spend in my wheelchair was quite limited in those early days, and it was estimated that in order to get home I would need to be able to tolerate being in it for 4-hour stretches, as that was the minimum time between visits I could expect from carers should we be using those when I did eventually get home. That seemed to be a remote possibility going by my earliest attempts. One day while Su was visiting me and I was sitting in it I frightened the life out of her by fainting after only quarter of an hour! Fortunately this was an isolated instance, but even on my better days I rarely managed more than an hour or so.

However, any progress that I was making came to a sudden standstill on the night between March 24th and 25th. All was apparently fine on the Tuesday evening (the 24th) as my visitors left shortly after eight o'clock and I settled down for sleep as usual. I've no recollection at all of what caused the panic but I remember nurses rushing backwards and forwards in the middle of the night and telling me they were getting a doctor to come and see me. Then they said they were moving me nearer the nurses' station so they could keep a closer eye on me. It seemed no time at all then before I was told I was being moved yet again, this time to my own room. At some stage I know that I evacuated my bowels quite violently – the phrase "up to my armpits" comes to mind but I couldn't say for certain how accurate that was, but my specialist nurse Clare had become involved by now and I remember her telling me that they would have to cut my pyjamas off me in order to clean me up. Su had been sent for and she got in touch with Christopher who picked her up and brought her in as it was clear that they were extremely concerned by this sudden downturn in my condition. Su decided she should also let

Rachael and Barbara know and it wasn't long before they both arrived as well. I knew I was in trouble then, but if there was any doubt at all it was dispelled by some bloke whose job it must have been to break the news to me. The comment which has remained with me ever since was "we would have put you on a ventilator but we didn't think you would survive!" Then he listed what alternative treatment they could offer, putting me on drips and this, that and something else. My mind was in a daze, barely able to take in what he'd said after that first sentence, so I just mumbled, "Run that past me again" and, sure enough, it still sounded as bad the second time around as it had the first time! So when he listed the alternatives again, I just said, "I think we'll go for that!"

The next thing I knew I was on my travels again as they wheeled me up to the Coronary Care Unit, that being where the machine I needed to help with my breathing was situated. I became quite reliant on that machine over the next few days as I was finding it very difficult to breathe without it. I cannot speak too highly of the treatment I received while I was on that ward. It was very quiet and peaceful there and the ratio of nurse to patient was almost one-to-one. The medical staff throughout my time in hospital were all really good with me, but their t.l.c. went up yet another notch in that ward. In addition every bed had its own telly with many extra channels included and it was free too – it was just a pity that most of the patients in there weren't well enough to watch it! I still don't think I was fully aware just how ill I was, but I suspect that may be nature's way of helping you to cope! However, despite their best ministrations my condition seemed to take a further downward turn on the Saturday morning, three days after being moved to that ward. The diagnosis was "pneumonia and septic shock" and this is such a lethal combination that I think they must have had serious doubts about my ability to recover from it. I felt dreadful and my spirits sank to a new low. It must have been apparent to the staff and one of the nurses asked if I'd like to see a priest. By this time I was ready to accept any help that might be going from whatever source, so I agreed. When Fr.Smith came he did his best to console me and I think he succeeded to some extent but I still spent the rest of the day not knowing what the future might hold for me, if indeed I had any future! My whole well-being over the last few years has been very up and down but I don't think I ever felt as bad at any time as I did that particular day. All I was able to do was pray, and I think I did that more strenuously than I have ever done, either before or since.

The change overnight was marked – all the negativity which had enveloped me the day before had disappeared and been replaced by a new sense of hope that maybe everything was going to be alright after all. I didn't know it at the time, as I was considered too ill to be told for a few days, but my dear brother Bob had died in the early hours of that Sunday morning. I make no claims that there was any connection between these two situations, but I can't help but think there may have been. All I know is that some strength came to me from somewhere, and I would like to think it may have been something to do with Bob and perhaps a positive response to my prayers.

Imagine what the rest of our family must have gone through at that time. It must have been incredibly traumatic as they had to come to terms with not just losing one member of the family but also with the distinct possibility that a second would follow, and when I survived they had to act for a few days as if their only concern was my well-being, and then break the news of Bob's death to me as delicately as possible. They succeeded admirably with all that they had to do, I never suspected anything until I was told, and when Su did tell me she did it perfectly. Quietly and quickly, as soon as she arrived on the Thursday following, she just said, "I have some bad news for you, we've lost Bob"! That was all it took, nothing more was needed. Obviously it was very emotional, and many more equally heartfelt meetings took place in the ensuing days and weeks as each member of the family came to see me. All were anxious to see how I would respond, while I was keen to show that I was coping if they were, and somehow we got through it. The funeral took place the following day after Su had told me, and it was arranged that the hospital chaplain would come to see me at some stage during the morning as I clearly wouldn't be able to go, but at least I would be with them in spirit.

I was gradually weaned off the magic machine as my condition started to improve and eventually I was able to breathe without any outside assistance, though I still had to have two tubes linked to oxygen tanks stuck up my nose for some weeks afterwards (the tubes, not the tanks!).

After ten days in the coronary care unit I was considered well enough to be moved into an interim ward where they would still be keeping an eye on me but without as much intensity as had to be the case in the CCU. I remember it was the weekend of the Grand National and one lively patient organised a sweep for patients, staff and visitors, everyone being invited to draw their horses out of a bedpan (unused!). If my memory serves me right, I have a sneaking suspicion that he actually won it, and he may even have got the runner-up as well!! Mmm! He managed to keep our spirits up with his antics, but he went home after a few days and I never really felt settled in this new ward, especially after his departure. Perhaps I'd been spoiled by my recent treatment, but the nurses didn't seem quite as sympathetic to us as I had grown accustomed to, so I was glad when they said they thought I was well enough to be moved back to Ribblesdale.

They made me very welcome back there again, I think most if not all of them thought when they'd moved me out of Ribblesdale that it was probably the last time they would ever see me, but like the proverbial bad penny there I was, back to torment and be tormented by them again!

The pneumonia had taken its toll on me, so I was continually being assessed for a while after my return, and they were particularly concerned about an amount of fluid which had been left on my lungs. So I had to undergo yet another procedure, this time to remove the aforementioned fluid. I was quite anxious about this, as I always was before they did anything new to me, but in reality it turned out to be no worse than the biopsy which Stuart had performed on me back in January. I had to keep the tube attached to me for a few days afterwards, until such time as it had drained as much as it was going to, and I recall Su being amazed at the quantity which appeared in the container as a result, I think it was more than a litre by the time it had done its job!

By this time the cricket season was well under way, and England were about to start a short Test series against the West Indies prior to the main event of the summer, the Ashes series against Australia. I knew I wouldn't be able to see much of the television coverage because of the limited choice of channels on Patientline and the fact that even the highlights programme on Channel 5 would clash with visiting times. I didn't think it would go down too well if I ignored my visitors in order to watch it so I was resigned to doing without. Alan saw it as an opportunity to do me a favour and he brought me a radio from home to enable me at least to listen to it even if I couldn't watch it. Unfortunately, though, we couldn't get any decent reception from it, possible because of the proximity of all the other electrical equipment around us. Undaunted, he went out and bought another one which the salesman assured him would be ok – it wasn't! Never mind, Alan – ten out of ten for effort anyway! At least I managed to see a lot of the Ashes coverage when that came around, but it took a major change in my circumstances to bring that about, but that change was waiting just around the corner...

It wasn't long before they started making those familiar noises again about me being discharged from hospital In theory this was exactly what I wanted to hear, but no progress had been made with regard to any alterations at home, and Su was still struggling with her hip, so it was clear that I still couldn't go there, which understandably was what I would have wanted. In truth, the alternative wasn't really on my list of desirable situations at all, but it became increasingly inevitable that I was going to end up being transferred to a nursing home.

Su was horrified when she was first confronted with this solution, on account of how she was convinced that I'd react to the suggestion. Every day on my way home from work I'd driven past the one which was the likeliest to be chosen, and it never entered my head that I might one day end up in there, and certainly not when I'd only just entered my sixth decade. By this time, though, I was getting desperate to escape from hospital, and even if this wasn't ideal, it would at least be a step in the right direction. It was only half a mile from home, so it would be easier for Su (and everyone else for that matter!) to visit. I would have my own room and as much privacy as I wanted, so it seemed a big improvement on what I had at the hospital. So it was arranged, but not before the powers that be at the hospital decided to give me one last tribulation before returning me to the real world – they transferred me from Ribblesdale Ward to Bleasdale Ward! I was told that this was a necessary stepping-stone on my way to leaving the hospital altogether but one of the nurses confided that really it was more of a dumping-ground where they put any patients they weren't sure what to do with!

Having said that, though, my stay there did get off to a promising start when I was put into my own room with a nice view of a garden outside, a view which one nurse claimed was the best in the whole hospital! The first problem with the ward arose when the bed that they put me in wasn't very comfortable as it hadn't got one of the special mattresses which I needed for my back. When I pointed this out I was told that they couldn't possibly do anything about it till the following day as by then it was about eight o'clock in the evening. Unusually for me I persisted and someone eventually agreed to see if anything could be done and it wasn't long before one was found for me. Incredibly, however, no offer came to fit it that night, until I reaffirmed that I couldn't do without it. Their body language left me in no doubt as to the reluctance of those concerned to fit it but at least they did. I would like to be able to say that that was the end of my problems but it wasn't, and that night was arguably the most uncomfortable one in all the five months I was in hospital. I spent a lot of sleepless hours interspersed with cries for help from me to the nurses on duty. It turned out that the mattress had been fitted the wrong way round and it was literally a great relief for me when the problem was resolved during the following morning. By that time, however, I had been removed from the comparatively luxurious surroundings of my own room and put into the general ward. At least my new position was by the window, even if the view was only of a car park.

Things did pick up somewhat after this initial setback and the staff attitude towards me improved as well, although there seemed to be a distinct tendency for a number of the younger ones to congregate in the general vicinity of my bed and either hold union-type meetings there or just have a general gossip, neither of which I would regard as 'professional' behaviour. I think they probably chose that place because it was situated furthest away from where their supervisors would be, but it might have been less of an issue had they held these get-togethers close to the beds of patients who were maybe not quite as "with it" as I would claim to be. It's a minor criticism of them, because I know they are hardly what you'd call overpaid for doing a difficult job which many people, myself included, would never have been able or willing to try.

It is entirely possible that by this time I was just more than ready for leaving hospital and I was at the stage where I was becoming a lot less tolerant of anything which I felt was not quite as it should be. Whatever the reason I think I was definitely becoming more like Mr.Grumpy with each passing day. I think I was the only patient in that part of the ward who was still "compos mentis", not to be confused with anyone at the other end of the scale, "compost mentis", or as it is colloquially known, "shit for brains"!

For a short time there was an old chap across from me who talked gibberish incessantly almost without pausing for breath. He would keep it up for about twenty minutes before subsiding into sleep, then without warning he'd be off again. He caused great amusement amongst many of the staff, and I could see the funny side of it at first. He seemed consumed with a strong dislike of Preston's number one all-time personality, ex-footballer Sir Tom Finney, but it wasn't his ability at sport that dominated his soliloquy. On the contrary listening to this chap you would never have known that Finney had been a sportsman at all as his whole spiel depicted him as a pervert preying on unsuspecting females. Let me just say that it was very graphic, and I'll leave the rest to your imagination! However, as I said, it was amusing, though sad, to hear it once, but when it was repeated hour after hour the novelty soon wore extremely thin. Fortunately (for me, anyway!), after a day of it they moved him somewhere else, so maybe that was their policy, to shift him every day before he drove everyone in the immediate vicinity as batty as he was!

Another old chap interrupted a conversation one visiting time when Su, Christopher and Rachael were with me and he asked if any of us spoke English! Christopher confirmed that we did, to which he then added his supplementary questions, "Do you think I'm horrid?" and "Why does nobody like me?"! Fortunately we were rescued by one of the nurses who came to walk him away, which he took to be a confirmation of the problems he thought he had!

So you can perhaps see why I was more than ready for my transfer, and even that didn't go as smoothly as we hoped when the fates contrived to delay us by a further day – not long by normal standards but when you're almost climbing the walls those twenty-four hours seemed interminable, but at last on Tuesday May 19th I left hospital and the ambulance took me to Cuerden Grange, my home for the next seven months...

John Blackburn

Part 2 – Nursing Home

Chapter 5

Home On The Grange!

It didn't take me long to settle in after my move to Cuerden Grange. It was like a home from home compared to life in hospital. It helps having your own room to start with, of course. We personalised it as far as we could. Su dug out the framed photograph of me crossing the finishing line in the Mersey Marathon back in 1987 and hung it on the wall, a permanent reminder that once upon a time I had actually managed to run/jog twenty-six miles even if my legs couldn't even support my weight now, let alone do a marathon.

Su and Christopher had been to the local Comet or Curry's and bought me a new television. There wasn't any Sky or cable TV at the Grange but as this set had built-in Freeview at least I could access a lot more channels than I could back in hospital, and at no extra charge as well! They brought bottles of beer to stock up the top shelf of my wardrobe (I didn't need much in the way of clothes so this seemed a far better use of the space!) and Alan contributed bottles of my other favourite tipples, whisky and brandy, as I sought to make up for lost time. It had become my oft-repeated claim while in hospital that I hadn't had a 'drink' since Christmas but had been legless since New Year, so I was keen to rectify that asap. I sought advice as I was still on quite a lot of medication, but it was agreed that it would probably do me more good than harm provided I didn't overdo it.

Apart from the alcohol, there were certain foods which I had been missing as they didn't supply them as part of the hospital's menu. I had been picturing them for weeks and promising that I would have them as soon as it was practical for me to do so. And what were these culinary delights? KFC, fried eggs with proper bacon, chips either made at home (no longer possible in ours as Su had disposed of our deep fat fryer whilst I was in hospital!) or from a chip shop, meat & potato pies and kebabs! As you will deduce from this list, I've always been a healthy eater! Before May was done I had managed to get everything on that list and my appetite was well and truly back, for a few months anyway.

The meals which they supplied at the Grange were okay, and I was very keen on them initially, especially as they were a vast improvement on the hospital fare, but it didn't take long before I started to go off them just as I had in hospital. As a result different members of the family would kindly call at takeaways for me on a regular basis. The problem was partially resolved once I progressed sufficiently to be allowed to go home for visits and Su made some meals for me then. But that was in the future – for the time being I had to get used to yet another set of routines as laid down by the 'powers-that-be' at Cuerden.

I had already met the lady in charge of Cuerden Grange, Diane, as she had been to see me in hospital to verify that I was a suitable candidate for their establishment and for her to confirm that they would be able to cope with whatever my needs might be while I was in their care. I was still unable to do much for myself apart from some basic ablutions and to feed myself. By this time I could manage an hour or so at a time out of bed in my wheelchair, so most days I was able to sit out for one of my meals during the day. Knowing in advance that the vast majority of other residents there would be considerably older than I was, I made it clear from the outset that I had no intention of mixing with the others. That sounds terribly selfish I know, and it isn't like me really, I am usually far more sociable than that, but the very thought of being surrounded by a lot of much older people whose minds may well be suffering at various stages of dementia and whose bodies might lack control of certain basic bodily functions was more than I felt I wanted to face on a regular basis. So if we were going to have to stump up more than £500 per week for the privilege of staying there, it was surely only right that I should be allowed to lay down a few ground rules of my own. To be fair they were very understanding from the start and never raised any objections. It was inevitable that our paths would cross from time to time, and I would become very aware of a lot of what was going on, especially on those odd occasions in the night when my door would slowly open and I'd be confronted by a confused resident not being able to find his/her way back to their room, but that was unavoidable. What I didn't want was a perpetual reminder of what might be in store for me in the future should I ever manage to get that far! As it was I saw and heard enough to be going on with, I assure you, or even to last a lifetime!

As a result of this attitude it follows that I didn't have any difficulty resisting invitations to join in with their occasional social events. Most of these were singalongs and they were held in the lounge/dining area only about ten yards up the corridor from my room so even though I wasn't participating I could always hear them. Mostly it seemed that a lot of the entertainment on offer was from singers encouraging them to sing along, mainly wartime songs as you might expect. In theory I would have loved to have asked if I could go along and tell a few jokes, though in my wheelchair that may well have made me the world's first ever sit down stand-up! The only reason I fancied that though was because I would love to have been able to use the opening line "If it's true that the good die young, there mustn't half be some evil bastards among you lot!" I suspect that that might not have been too well received though…!

My timetable wasn't an awful lot different from what it had been in the Royal Preston, so it didn't take much to get used to it and it wasn't long before I felt I'd been there for ages. I had to take one of my tablets about seven o'clock in the morning, an hour or two before I ate anything, so that became my regular wake-up call. The shifts changed over at half past seven and a number of the incoming staff tended to congregate in the corridor fairly close to my room, so their chatter ensured I didn't usually go back to sleep. It didn't greatly bother me though as I knew I'd almost certainly be catching up on any missed shuteye after breakfast!

I abandoned my trusty standby from my hospital days, cornflakes, when I went to Cuerden, as the lure of a cooked breakfast was too much to resist, especially after being denied it throughout my five months in Royal Preston. The regular type of egg on offer was poached, but they said I could have my preferred choice of fried if I wanted, so that's what I had, provided whoever was on duty remembered! Bacon was the usual accompaniment, of course, but early on I did have sausage as well until one day I decided I didn't really like the ones on offer. Oh what a fussy bugger I am!

Right, breakfast out of the way, what shall I do today? I know, I'll have a sleep on it while I await my carers coming in for my morning wash! And that's what I did most mornings – not very much, to be honest! In fact, even less than not very much – sweet F.A. if we are being totally truthful, and that's not a reference to the Football Association!

A great deal of my time was actually spent sending text messages, mainly to Su but also to anyone else who might be in my list of contacts. Whatever did we do before the advent of mobile phones? They do have a negative aspect, of course, and anyone reliant on public transport doesn't need me to remind them about being subjected to the incessant varied and often bizarre ringtones and the peculiar conversations which they are frequently made to overhear whether they want to or not. For me, though, my phone was a godsend throughout 2009 and I don't know what I would have done without it. Before I went into hospital I did carry it about with me but hardly ever used it. How that changed when I was admitted into Royal Preston! The tariff which I was on was totally unsuitable for my new situation as I was on 'pay as you go' and that meant I was paying for every single text I sent. By the time I transferred to Cuerden Grange I was sending hundreds each month so it was fortunate for me that Su had sorted out a proper arrangement with the phone company even though it meant I was then under contract, something which I had previously not wanted.

Obviously I received myriad texts too and I felt as if it really kept me in contact with the outside world. A number of these messages I have kept and looking at them serves to remind me of the various stages I went through that year and the support which I had from so many friends and family members

Su was the one with whom I exchanged the most texts, as you would expect, but most days began with one from Rachael as she wished me "Good morning" on her way to work on the bus which went past the Grange, and she usually remembered to send me one last thing at night as well. I always wondered if maybe something was wrong if I didn't get my routine reassurance from her.

The one drawback with this was the consequential dependence on it and hence the panic which inevitably ensued when I didn't receive a message at a time when one was expected and, heaven forbid, on the couple of occasions when I mislaid my phone! I became extremely reliant on it and as I've always been a worrier any delay invariably led to me believing something dreadful must have happened which fortunately it never had – up to now anyway!

Most of the carers were quite a jolly bunch, and this is very much to their credit because they weren't very well paid and some of the treatment they received from certain other residents was atrocious. Without blowing my own trumpet too much I think they appreciated the times when I was included on their 'to do' list. More often than not I would give them a warm welcome and I did at least appreciate what they did for me. I even got round to telling some of them jokes when I got to know them better, but I suppose it's debatable whether that's a plus or not, though in my defence I can claim that odd ones amongst them used to seek me out to ask me to tell more, believe it or not! Yes, they were a whole new audience for me, having exhausted my family, friends and workmates with my attempts at humour over the years.

Some of them also talked about their home lives, in the same way as you might with any friend, because in time that's what we were. They knew a fair amount about me so it was a natural progression that our conversations would lead to me learning bits about them as well. This did lead to problems on occasions, however, when they possibly gave me more information than maybe they should have, at least in the eyes of the management. So when one of them got injured when she fell off a table while dancing at a club during a staff night out, having over-indulged with the liquid refreshment, she ended up in even more trouble when it was discovered that word had got to me about it! Quite why it should matter to the management that I should have learned of it quite escapes me, but I gather they are supposed to keep themselves detached from residents and presumably only converse about matters directly related to them and their needs. I considered it quite pathetic and was more than happy to share that opinion with anyone prepared to listen!

I usually got hoisted out of bed after my wash and into my wheelchair for a few hours if I felt up to it. When I was feeling really daring and adventurous I might go for a ride up and down the corridor in a vain attempt to build up my arm muscles in order to give me some small level of independence. I had occasional visits from a physio, Gill, and she gave me some arm exercises to do using a length of stretchy rubber. I'd like to say that as a result my muscles grew noticeably but I'm afraid that hasn't been the case, they remain as puny as ever. Still, I don't suppose you can expect to have brawn as well as brains and beauty, can you? Mind you, one out of the three would have been quite useful...!

As with my time in hospital, visiting was inevitably the focal point of every day. I've already mentioned that Su came to see me every day in hospital and this continued when I moved to the Grange, except for the period in July when she herself was hospitalised, having her second hip replacement, and for a short while after her return home. The boot was on the other foot when I actually managed to visit her while she was in hospital! Christopher arranged for one of those taxis which can accommodate someone in a wheelchair to pick us up at the Grange and take us to visit and bring us back after, and using the same mode I was able to go to watch my football team for the first time for twenty months at the start of the new season. That's when I really knew that significant steps were being taken with my progress.

While in hospital I hadn't shown any interest in doing anything much, apart from reading the morning paper bought from Mr.Squeakie and Su would bring me the local evening paper which we have delivered at home, and Barbara used to bring the weekly Chorley Guardian too. There wasn't very much room for things to be brought in, just what could be fitted on my over-the-bed table. I often seemed to be in dispute with various people as to what I was allowed to have on my table, everyone wanted to throw things away or rearrange them, but I had everything positioned just as I wanted and resisted all their attempts at getting me to change what I did. Adding anything else would just have created more problems, so I decided not to accept Su's many offers to bring in my laptop or personal DVD player and the only exception I made was for my MP3 player.

All that changed once I got to the Grange – bring it all on! All the electrical gadgets just listed were brought in and suddenly I was back in business. Having also been amply supplied with liquid refreshment of an alcoholic kind, I now started to feel that I really was back in the land of the living at last!

Apart from Su's daily calls, I also had a steady stream of visitors, much as I had while in hospital, and it was always a delight to see friends from work and fellow football supporters to supplement the family visits. People tend to be surprised that despite my many years working for the library service I have never really been an avid reader. I've usually got one book 'on the go' but it usually takes me an age to read it right through. I did manage to finish two though while at Cuerden – Stuart Maconie's Pies and Prejudice and Frank Skinner's autobiography. That should give you some idea of my literary taste, though I am also partial to books like Eats Shoots and Leaves by Lynne Truss and James Cochrane's 'Between You And I'. I have recently finished one which Su bought me for Christmas, 'I Before E Except After C', as a result of which I can now spell diarrhoea with confidence, plus I know what and when the signs of the Zodiac are and the order of the planets in relation to the sun, not forgetting the names for all the different-sized bottles of champagne! If a little knowledge is indeed a dangerous thing, you have every reason to be wary of me, I assure you!

I started to do a bit of writing again once I got back into the swing of it. I've always felt it's what I wanted to do and I've dabbled with it on and off throughout my life. An English teacher at school had given me some encouragement and once told one of my fellow pupils that I was the only one in the school who could successfully incorporate humour into essays! Quite a tribute coming from someone whose opinion I valued and as you now know one which has stayed with me all my life. Whether you agree with his assessment or not though is not for me to decide though, is it?!

Unfortunately I have never found it easy to stick with any project through to its conclusion, so I have very little to show for my efforts over the years. I've been working on a story about the four years I spent in my teens training to be a member of a religious order, but that's been ongoing for over twenty years and still shows no signs of being completed! It was always my hope and intention that I would possibly finish it off once I retired, so you never know, I really do hope I'm able to complete it one day. Then there was the time after I'd run the marathon, I thought I could write a basic instruction manual for any budding joggers on the basis that if I could run one anybody could! I did finish that one but it was only about 120 pages long and when I wrote to a few agents I couldn't get anybody to take any interest at all. I ended up contacting a local publisher who did make a few encouraging noises so I sent him a copy of the manuscript and never heard anything again! As good as that, eh?! His publishing company disappeared without trace too, never to be heard of again, and I still have visions of him doing a moonlight flit clutching a copy of my manuscript in his little mits as he sped off into the night!

On a smaller scale, for a number of years now I have written articles for my football team's programme, and before my illness I used to write reports on their matches for the local newspaper. There has never been any realistic possibility that I would resume that even if they wanted me to, as the chemo drugs have caused my eyesight to deteriorate significantly and I doubt that my concentration would be good enough now either, but I have started to submit articles for the programme again so that at least helps me to keep my "hand in". In total I didn't really do a lot of writing while at the Grange, but what little I did at least served the purpose of getting me back into the habit of doing some, if only a bit at a time.

I watched quite a lot of television in the evenings in those early days and also got into the habit of watching DVDs on my laptop in the early hours. As I wasn't waking up properly until late morning, and not expending much energy even then, I wasn't particularly tired at night so I welcomed all the diversions I could glean from my electronic gadgets. It became normal practice for me to watch either a film or concert or sporting event on disc until one or two o'clock in the morning, then transfer my headphones to my MP3 player and spend another hour or two listening to the music on that, often until I dozed off, and even later. It wasn't unusual for me to come to about five o'clock and have to switch the MP3 player off! I found that this was a very good way for me to drown out most of the unwanted noises coming from elsewhere in the building!

It seems strange but I think I can see why one tends to get closer to night staff in places like this. In the same way that I became good friends with Lisa T while I was in hospital, so it was at the Grange that I got quite pally with a few of their night carers and nurses, and chief amongst those was yet another Lisa. This in no way minimises the contribution made by either the day staff (so apologies to Val, Tracey, Sarah, Amanda. Lisa S, Jenny, Karyn, Arifa and the rest of you lovely people!) or the others who worked nights, but Lisa Metcalfe was a larger than life character who lightened many a dark night, often with the help of her co-conspirators Irene and Annette.

The daytime at hospital and at Cuerden was always a hive of activity and staff only have a limited amount of time they can spend with you before they are likely to be needed elsewhere. At night it was different – once all the residents had been settled they were left to their own devices, provided they were available for any incidents which might arise during the night. So we used to have a few laughs, let's put it that way! Nothing unprofessional and certainly neither illegal or immoral either, but just a few laughs! Lisa gave us a few unintended chuckles along the way too, like the night I introduced her to Barbara, telling her at the same time that she was my twin sister. "Are you identical?" she asked without batting an eyelid, and I don't think you need to see photographs of us to realise how wrong she just had to be, but if you are unsure I refer you to the family photo as featured within these pages which was taken on the occasion of our sixtieth birthday – she is the one sat down without a beard! On another occasion, and it may be that I am being ultra-critical of her here in this digital age, but I couldn't believe it when we had to explain to her what the word 'clockwise' meant! I can't forget, either, the night I buzzed for someone to bring the hoist for me so that I could use the commode and Lisa came to sort me out but forgot to make sure there was a bucket in the commode before she left me to get on with my business! I had no idea that it wasn't there as I am not blessed with a third eye (!) till she came back after the performance! Fortunately all involved were able to see the funny side of it…!

Lisa was also very much into ghosts and haunted houses and one night she and Julie, one of the nurses at Cuerden, went to the Winter Gardens theatre in Morecambe, which is supposed to be haunted, to spend a night there. She came back the following night full of it and so one of the staff who shall remain nameless in case this gets read by someone in authority and gets her into trouble hid in one of the empty rooms with a sheet over her head then jumped out making appropriate ghostly noises just as Lisa was walking down the corridor! Well, in a place like that you have to make your own entertainment or you'd end up as batty as some of the residents!

I feel that I may be doing Lisa something of a disservice by focussing on her scattiness at the expense of trying to get across how kind she was. She used to go to the local 'chippy ' for us on a Friday and we'd share a fish'n'chip supper. Also she knew how concerned I was about Su walking home on her own especially at the time when it was such a physical struggle for her, and Lisa used to look out for her and give her a lift home whenever she could. It's little things like that that you don't forget.

Chapter 6

Home Visits

Once I had managed a couple of trips away from the Grange, and Su was on the road to recovery from her op, there seemed to be no reason why I shouldn't be able to try home visits. All I needed was some fine weather and a few volunteers prepared to push me the half mile home and back again after tea. And that's where my oldest friend Ian Hyde really came into his own...

My brother Alan and son Christopher along with a few other friends all came and did their bit when they could. There was one memorable journey when Alan was struggling to push me through the doors of the Grange up the hill to the main road and the strains of a hit song from yesteryear floated out from behind us – it was the Hollies singing "He Ain't Heavy, He's My Brother", a sentiment which Alan Blackburn certainly did not share with Allan Clarke at that particular moment!

However, Ian's personal circumstances meant that he was able to make himself available not just round the clock, but round the calendar as well, and he did! He and his wife

Eileen had come to visit me in hospital as soon as they heard I was in there and they were regular visitors, and always came bearing gifts. Also, being aware that Su is a non-driver, they insisted on being regular taxi drivers for her too.

It may not have been a good day for Ian when he was made redundant around the same time that I was moved to Cuerden, but Su and I have had many a reason to be thankful for his early retirement as he has been a tower of strength to us ever since. As well as all the lifts he has given us he's also done odd jobs for us and made it clear that he would do whatever we might want, and he never even added the usual proviso "just so long as it's legal and moral"!

Having written what would surely be a worthy character reference for anyone, we were all shattered last year to be given the devastating news that Ian himself was diagnosed with cancer too! In typical Ian fashion he has done his best to make light of the situation, on the one hand saying that he was thinking of telling people that he has got a tropical disease which "isn't Capricorn", then on the other suggesting that he thinks he might have caught it from me!

I'm pleased to be able to say that his attitude towards it is very positive, and the prognosis certainly suggests that he has every reason to be. He had to endure something like eight hours surgery followed by two weeks in hospital and was then allowed back home to recuperate. It was estimated that his recovery may take up to six months, but we are well past that now and he is still suffering from various symptoms. He also had to endure six solid weeks of radiotherapy which I know was far more painful than I had to endure but hopefully he is now over the worst and time will prove to be a great healer for him.

It all sounded very daunting to me when he told me what he was going to have done, because in my case I didn't have time to get worked up about my diagnosis before it was on me. I dread to think how I might have reacted had I been faced with his situation, but I can guarantee it wouldn't have been anything like as well as he has. Back in those Cuerden days, though, he was such a good friend to me and became my most regular "pusher"!

Before I could be allowed home, even just to visit, certain preparations had to be made. There wasn't any access to our house for a wheelchair until our occupational therapist Joanne set things in motion and a temporary platform was built at the front of the house to which could be placed ramps for me to be wheeled up. These had to be detachable because we have a shared drive and it wouldn't have been possible for our next-door neighbours to get their car(s) on to it with ramps permanently in place. Once all that was sorted it only remained to check that I was in a fit state to make the journey. Obvious things like making sure I was warm enough and had any medication with me that might be needed while on my travels readily spring to mind, but the matter of toileting became the most important concern and the area which would cause the most problems. Bear in mind that I had to be hoisted everywhere whether that was from bed to wheelchair, wheelchair to bath or toilet and you can possibly imagine potential areas of difficulty. I wouldn't be able to get up our stairs while at home and we didn't have any facilities downstairs. Ideally, of course, it would have been good if I could have used the loo before we left to come home and hope that I would then be ok till I got back. Good idea in theory but couldn't be relied on as a foolproof plan. I had been catheterised for part of the time I had been in hospital, and supplied with a bottle for the rest of the time, and it was this latter method which we used at the Grange. I would like to say that that was perfect but it wasn't – the profile bed that I had to sleep in was electric with a special air mattress to ease the pressure on my back, so when I moved, so did the mattress. This was all very strange at first but quite comfortable and beneficial for me in the long run, though not conducive to using these bottles. I'll have to leave some of this to your imagination but suffice to say that for efficient use the top of the bottle needs to be higher than the bottom (the bottle's bottom, that is, not mine!) when it is in use, otherwise any liquid would come back out as soon as it went into the bottle, but the mattress didn't always allow this to happen, so accidents were always possible. Clearly what I'm saying to you is that any failure with these was never my fault, and that is my story and I'm sticking to it!

But I digress – attempts were made to find alternative ways of dealing with this, mainly by use of what they called uridoms which, as their name suggests, fit like condoms but are for use in assisting the male appendage with its non-sexual function! They would be useless as condoms because they have a hole at the other end! This is then attached to a tube leading to a bag which has a tap to allow it to be emptied easily. Brilliant – in theory! Sadly, though, not foolproof, and no prizes for guessing who the fool was who proved it!

The initial problem stems from the state of the organ on which the uridom is to be placed. It doesn't take a great deal of imagination to appreciate why this would be easier with a condom, but to make it easier to keep the uridom on they have a kind of glue on the inside to hopefully hold them in place when in position. Unfortunately this is a bit of a hit-and-miss affair – sometimes you're lucky, sometimes you're not, sometimes they stick and sometimes they don't! It may be ok when you first put it on but any force when in use could easily cause it to fail and come unstuck. Not only that but also, being glued, it could be quite a painful process removing them from such a tender part of one's anatomy!

They also come in different sizes which caused many a chuckle and plenty of innuendo too! I can still see the look on Lisa's face the night she came in to my room and announced that she had to measure me! What did I tell you about pride and dignity flying out of the window as soon as you pass through the door of either a hospital or nursing home?! It wouldn't really serve any purpose if I told you the results of her measuring, but let me just say that if there was a sliding scale ranging from Action Man's lack of anything to denote why he isn't called Action Person up to the legendary King Dong who allegedly could wrap his equipment round his legs(!), my measurements would be much closer to the former than the latter! Not to worry, if my pride was slightly dented as a consequence of this procedure, perhaps I could at least be compensated to a degree with the knowledge that maybe some of my carers went home more appreciative of what they had waiting for them there!

However, don't get me started about the other side of toileting! This was hopefully not going to be a problem and most of the time it wasn't. If I needed to go in the time leading up to my excursion I could be hoisted on to a commode as usual, and I should then be okay until I got back at night. But nature doesn't always act to order, does it, so there was never any guarantee that our hopes and expectations in this regard would be realised? In practice there were only a couple of instances where we experienced difficulties with this, but believe me they are etched on my mind clearly, never to be erased! We must have been quite a sight as I was pushed at great speed on the road back to Cuerden like a scene from the Keystone Cops, desperate to get back before severe embarrassment might have been the least of my problems. As luck would have it, I did manage to hang on for the duration of both these journeys, but it possibly did owe more to good luck than good management on my part!

This isn't a subject on which I would want to dwell any longer than is necessary, so all I'll say in conclusion and by way of summing up what I feel on this topic is this – never underestimate the pleasure of a successful no.2! You spend so much of your life taking it for granted that it's only when you have problems in that area that you really appreciate it and it's too late then. What comes to mind now is that birthday card or email giving advice to people who are, let's just say, getting on a bit. Three rules they say you should live by – don't go past the loo without calling in, don't trust a fart and never waste an erection! Well I have now learnt to live by two of those rules, you'll have to guess which ones they are, and in the words of the old Meatloaf song, "Two out of three ain't bad!"

It did me the world of good to be able to get home on these visits, a change of scene from the four walls I had in my room at the Grange, to be back in my own home surroundings again, if only for a few hours. We didn't do much on these occasions, I was happy just to savour the peace and quiet and to watch a bit of television. A few of my visits coincided with the Ashes being played in this country at the time, so that was a welcome boost for me because I couldn't watch it at Cuerden as it was only available on Sky. Another great plus for me was a return to being able to benefit from a bit of home cooking, as Su ensured that I had a proper tea before my chauffeur/pusher came to take me back. All very cosy, but just as I was settling in to the routine of these regular home visits fate was waiting to deal me yet another slap in the face...

Chapter 7

Yet Another Setback, Then Good News At Last!

"Shingles!" The doctor only spoke one word when he came to look at the rash which had suddenly appeared on my back, but it spoke volumes as it confined me to bed for weeks afterwards and set my progress back immeasurably.

I hadn't been aware that there was anything the matter with me, but one of the carers caught sight of it as I was being put to bed for the night and after consulting the nurse on duty suggested they should send for the doctor. I agreed, having no suspicion what the verdict might be, though the staff at Cuerden told me later that they were fairly certain that that was what it was.

As I didn't feel particularly unwell at that early stage I persuaded them to let me go home for my next visit but I soon had cause to ask Alan to come to pick me up early and take me back as presumably the shingles started to take effect. Once he got me back to Cuerden I didn't get out of bed for three weeks, apart from being hoisted for necessary toilet visits. The rash spread till it was covering a quarter of my back then round the front down into the groin area. None of the staff had ever seen such a severe case, indeed some of the younger ones hadn't seen any case at all, but it soon became very painful and had to be treated as if it was a burn. That was how it felt too, I had to have the dressings changed and a very cold cream gently applied every four hours, and at least that relieved it, if only briefly. One of the girls asked me if she could take a picture of my back, so I let her, but only on my phone. If I look at the photograph now, it's a bit blurred and not very graphic, in fact you probably wouldn't even know what it was if you hadn't been told in advance, but believe me it was very painful and I wouldn't wish it on anyone. I believe it's not uncommon for people to have it round their head, in their hair and, God forbid, in their eyes! My heart goes out to anyone who has suffered like that because, horrid though mine was, I think the pain I endured would have paled into insignificance compared to what they must have to go through.

I had only been able to sleep on my back all year but felt the time was ripe to at least try to spend some time on one side or the other, which hopefully would then give me the added benefit of easing the pain from the shingles. Had the affected area been on my front I could have stayed on my back and been prescribed Viagra to ease the pain. Are you ahead of me here or are you querying "Why Viagra"? In case you haven't worked it out, it would have been to enable me to lift the bedclothes away from my body and keep them there without needing to use my hands!

Eventually the pain eased and the shingles became slightly less visible, but their effects lingered on, and on, and on. There is a condition known as post-herpetic neuralgia, which means that the nerve-endings which the shingles attack can remain affected for a long time afterwards. This has been the case with me, and I'm still not completely free from it more than two years later. I refer to it as the "shingle tingle" which I feel describes it as accurately as its official name! I've learned to live with it and am just glad that it's not any more severe than it is, because at its peak it really was extremely painful.

All this took place between late September and early December and it was so good after all that had happened that eventually I was able to resume my visits home. I was also, at last, able to celebrate a very good piece of news which I had received within a couple of days of starting with the shingles. My latest blood test had shown that my cancer was in remission! I'm sure you can imagine how that feels, but it was most unfortunate that I wasn't able to fully appreciate it at the time as by then I was succumbing to the full effects of the shingles. It didn't mean that I was cured because, as I had been told at the outset, myeloma isn't curable, but it did at least show that the chemotherapy I had had had done what it was supposed to do, and I do believe that is the first time I've ever written a sentence using the word 'had' three times in a row, and it not be wrong!

I would still have to have regular blood tests and go to hospital for checkups, but the initial crisis was definitely behind us and perhaps we would still have quite a few more tomorrows to look forward to. It also opened up the possibility of my having other treatments which could maybe extend my life expectancy a bit further, like a stem cell transplant, for instance. But more of that later. For the time being I had had more than enough of hospitals, thankyou very much, and just wanted to savour each day on its own merits.

I was still having to be hoisted everywhere, of course, as any attempts to progress had been put on hold while I was suffering from the shingles, but once I had started to get my home visits back on track again, my physio Gill thought it might be a good time for her to introduce me to the banana board! This was neither yellow nor edible, and all that it had in common with the fruit was its shape. Even there, though, it only bore a passing resemblance as it was considerably larger than any banana I had ever seen, and flat! But I was told it was called a banana board regardless of my reservations about its name and it turned out to be a simple but invaluable aid to my progress, even though half the time the carers would refer to it as the " banana boat" to cries of "Dayo, day dayo, daylight come and me wanna go home" in true Harry Belafonte style!

The purpose of this board was to bridge the gap between two surfaces, as for instance between my bed and my wheelchair. Presuming that I wanted to get from the former to the latter, one end of the board was put on the edge of the bed, the other resting on the wheelchair. My job was to manoeuvre myself so that my rear end was on the board on the bed, then slide myself along the board till I was in the chair. As luck would have it I seemed to be able to do this without too much difficulty and it wasn't long before I was able to build on that initial success and I started to bring it home on my visits so that instead of having to sit in my wheelchair all the time I was at home I could spend the afternoon in my reclining chair – result! Su wondered whether I might be able to get from my bed to a commode using this board as well but the Grange didn't have one with movable arms to make it possible. However, Diane agreed to buy one as she could see it as being of benefit to them in the longer term. This meant that I hardly needed to be hoisted anywhere after that which was a huge step in the right direction for me.

This got even better following a suggestion from another friend, Phil, who also happens to be my optician and has been for more than forty years. He had offered to give me a push home in the wheelchair, but when he saw what we were doing with the banana board, he wondered if I might be able to get in and out of a car using the same method. By this time I was happy to try anything that might help to improve my situation so we had a go and probably because the seats in his car were at a higher level than most it worked. Suddenly all sorts of things seemed possible – trips home were easier and quicker, no longer subject to the weather, and there was also the potential to go on shortish car journeys too. I still couldn't manage great distances as I wasn't particularly comfortable and my body would seize up if I stayed in the same position too long, but this latest move undoubtedly constituted a major breakthrough.

By the middle of December it was decided that there would be a meeting at our house of the different professional people who were involved in my case, plus Su and me. There was our occupational therapist Joanne, a social worker (yet another Lisa!) and Gill the physio, all there to see what was best for me and how we might progress. Su and I certainly weren't prepared for what came out of the meeting – Joanne, who had been leading the discussion, suddenly announced out of the blue that she couldn't see any reason why I shouldn't be able to come home – permanently! Not only that, but she reckoned that if she tried really hard getting everything together that would be needed, she could get it all in place so that I could be home in time for Christmas! Bloody hell!!! What a present that would be!

What a long way we'd come in the last few months, especially bearing in mind the setback with the shingles. No alterations had been done to the house apart from the platform outside the front door. Su had had meetings with an architect and all sorts of fancy things had been suggested, but any of them would have needed planning permission, and consequently a great deal of time and expense. As a result, no firm decisions had been taken, yet here we were being offered the chance of getting me back home without any major alterations having to be done or any great financial outlay on our part. It meant us losing the dining part of our kitchen/dining area as that is where my bed would have to be, but that seemed a small price to pay if it meant I could actually get back under my own roof to stay!

What a hive of activity our house was in the ensuing week, Su as ever at the heart of the operation. As well as preparing the house for the arrival of all the equipment I would need, she also arranged for someone to come and measure up for blinds to ensure I would have the necessary privacy in my new bedroom.. He arrived the following Monday just as the bed was being assembled so that he had almost to clamber over everything to do what was needed. Invaluable assistance from Christopher and friends had ensured the dining-room table had been safely removed to the garage in good time. As a result, as well as the bed and luxury mattress there was the rather large stand-aid to help me do as its name suggests. I had only just started to use one of those in my last couple of weeks at Cuerden and its very presence was significant in showing what progress I was starting to make, not having been able to stand at all throughout the year. Then there was the essential commode as doubtless you'll recall we have no toilet facilities downstairs.

Everything, then, was in place and in working order ready for me to come home on that Tuesday morning,

December 22nd. All that was missing was an over-the-bed table but that came under the heading 'desirable' rather than 'essential' so we said we would happily wait and manage without that until such time as one could be supplied.

The truth is that I would happily have come home on the Monday once I heard that everything was ready, and Ian had said he would gladly come for me if it could be arranged but Su felt it would be better to leave the arrangements as they were for a number of reasons so I reluctantly complied. What's another day anyway and in truth I couldn't have gone home until the evening and as I was scheduled to go the morning after it meant there was only about half a day I would have to wait and for the largest part of that I would be asleep so the gain for me would have been minimal. As it turned out, however, that single day did make a significant difference for us, and left us wishing it had been possible for me to come home on the Monday. Apart from my obvious eagerness to get home as soon as possible, another reason for suggesting the earlier day was that as everything was ready there wasn't any need for me to stay at Cuerden for another day, when the cost there per day was over £70. What we weren't aware of, though, was that my coming home on a Tuesday would have further detrimental financial implications for us. I still find it incredible to believe that this is what happened, but it did!

As I still needed round-the-clock assistance, Su became my nominated carer, and she was entitled to be paid for carrying out such duties as might be expected from a carer, because had she not been there someone else would have had to step into that position. The amount she was paid was not particularly generous but it was better than nothing. However, we soon learned that all payments were made from the start of the week so if, as was the case with us, one came under the auspices of a carer on a Tuesday, she didn't get paid until the following week! How ridiculous is that?! Theoretically, it meant that there was nobody being paid to look after me for the first six days I was at home, and that was Christmas week – what did they think that I was going to do? Was the baby Jesus going to use his miraculous powers to enable me to look after myself for a week, or was Santa going to come down the chimney and present me with a new fully functional body? I don't think so!

In some ways I'm overstating our case as it's only fair to point out that in my first few weeks at home I did have assistance from other quarters. A care package was put in place so that I was entitled to have a team of carers from an agency to come to me up to four times a day. These would coincide roughly with mealtimes, so they would come and get me up in the morning, help with washing and dressing, and prepare any meals too if needed. In reality we only used the one visit per day from then, the morning one, reasoning that Su would be able to help me for the rest of the day.

However, this does not minimise the fact that if they were prepared to pay Su for acting as my carer, why would they not start paying her from the day she took on the job? To compound that, they only paid her from then until early April when she turned sixty, even though she has carried on doing exactly the same things for me since. The whole system defies logic in my humble opinion, and seems to me to be patently unfair. Having said all that, though, I know that Su would have carried out all the tasks she did whether they had paid her or not, as indeed she did that first week and has done ever since she turned sixty!

Right, that's got all the negatives out of the way, almost everything else has been positive since then. When I woke up on the Tuesday morning, I had my last Cuerden breakfast then waited as patiently as I could for someone to come and help me as usual with my morning wash, and they kindly stayed around to bag up everything that I had there to bring home with me. As soon as seemed appropriate I sent Ian a text telling him I was ready to be picked up whenever it was convenient for him. It had started to snow and by the time he arrived for me there was quite a significant layer of it on the ground. But no way was that going to stop me – as long as it was ok for Ian, it was certainly fine by me. He loaded his car up with my goods and chattels and we were on our way – home at last!

Charlie aged 3 months

…and at 10 months!

…standing up(praying for granddad?!)

Wedding bells – Christopher & Alison tie the knot!

L toR – Rosie (Alison's stepdaughter), Rachael, Nancy (Alison's mother), Mr. & Mrs.Blackburn Jr. & Charlie, Mr. & Mrs.Blackburn Sr.

The calm before the storm! With Su January 2008 (My 60th Birthday)

Part 3 – Home, Sweet Home!

Chapter 8

2010, A Year Of Progress!

What an enjoyable Christmas that turned out to be, to bring to an end on a more positive note the hardest year in my whole life, despite the fact that I hadn't had to do any work at all during the whole year. What made it even more special was that really it was most unexpected. The prospect until a week before it happened was that we were working out how I could manage to come home for at least a couple of hours at some stage on Christmas Day, yet here I was home with all my immediate family for the whole day!

I was going to say that it's the first time we've had our Christmas dinner on laptrays but that's not strictly true as that was how I had eaten my minimal festive meal the year before. We managed anyway and for me it was truly a time to count my blessings.

By the time the New Year dawned we had begun to settle on a new routine. A couple of carers would arrive some time between 10 and 11 to get me up for my wash and to get me dressed and once they had ensured I was safely into my wheelchair that was it for them for the day as far as I was concerned. I'd spend an hour or two in the wheelchair before transferring to my recliner. In the course of the day I would do some of the exercises with the stretchy band which Gill the physio had left me and we bought some small ankle weights to help me do some leg-strengthening work. I had started to test myself a little in my latter days at Cuerden, taking my weight on my arms as I attempted to raise myself up a little bit out of my chair. On the odd home visit I made occasional attempts to stand up at the sink, and we regarded that as quite a breakthrough, even though the length of time I could hold the position was only 10-15 seconds.

From those small beginnings, though, 2010 became a year of great progress. After a few weeks of the basic care package it was decided that I was ready to attempt a few weeks of exercises with a different set of carers whose job it was to help me to improve what I could already actually do. They were rehab carers and would be working with me for six weeks to see what further improvements they could help me to make. I managed a few steps on my own using a Zimmer frame and in time it was felt that I was ready to attempt a few stairs. So, holding on to the bannister for dear life I managed to hoist myself up one step, then it was two, three and four, and I also succeeded in coming down them as well, though without turning round. At the time I couldn't bear the thought of trying to come down them forwards without feeling somewhat faint. I was also given a perching stool in the hope that perhaps at some stage I would be able to sit at the sink to have my wash or even at the work surface in the kitchen to do some basic tasks.

The four steps twice and a walking tour of our downstairs, i.e. our lounge and kitchen/dining-room/my bedroom, with the frame was the sum total of what the carers were allowed to do with me, but it wasn't long before I reasoned that if I could manage what they were asking me to do there was nothing really to stop me from going all the way up the stairs as there were only twelve of them in total. So one brave day after they had gone I attempted it, and it wasn't anything like as difficult as I had expected, though I was somewhat exhausted once I'd got back down again, taking each step backwards. It would be a long time before I'd be able to come back down forwards in the more conventional manner.

Cue the need now for extra equipment – a second walking frame arrived for use upstairs, together with a raised toilet seat and frame to help me get on and off the loo, and a special seat for the bath too so that I could sit on it and be lowered into the water and out again. Then there was a contraption for the bed to automatically raise my head from the horizontal position at the touch of a button, and vice versa.

This ability to get up and down the stairs and be able to sleep in my own bed again and use our own bathroom as well was an enormous boost to my system, and something which I had never dared believe would ever happen. I've mentioned my old friend Bob from work in a previous context, and one of his sayings was, usually when talking about coming home after a holiday, "You can't beat your own bed and your own bog!" How true!

Before I knew it Joanne the OT was here again, this time helping me to step outside the house. Then the carers had me doubling up what I had been doing with them, going up and down my four stairs twice and a couple of laps of our downstairs with the frame. This Zimmer frame had arrived to take the place of the stand-aid which in truth never got used for the purpose for which it was intended, not by me anyway, as I had started to stand up using my own way at the sink or in my wheelchair. Not that it wasn't used at all – it came in very handy to stand my telly on so that I could watch comfortably while in bed, but that didn't really justify us hanging on to it once it became apparent that it wasn't really needed. It was a bit on the large side too so we welcomed the extra space we gained when it was taken away.

It wasn't long before I was also able to dispense with the "bed-aid" or "sit-u-up" as I think it was called, then the Zimmer frames went too, to be replaced by a pair of elbow crutches and that's about as far as we've got up to now. We've had a stairlift fitted for days when I'm not really fit enough to use the stairs myself, so I've had to put up with all the comments you might expect to do with this and the wheelchair. Comparisons with Phoenix Nights' Brian Potter and Little Britain's Andy Pipkin are commonplace, and I don't suppose I did myself any favours when Ian wheeled me into Asda to try and find a birthday card for Su and as soon as we reached the card section I pointed to the first one I came across and said, "I want that one!" "But that's a sympathy card!" "I know…!"

Even worse than these comedy comparisons has been the suggestion that my attempts at walking are not unlike Julie Walters' elderly waitress in the famous Victoria Wood sketch! It does mean, though, that when I get to where I am going I can't resist asking in a very shaky voice, "Are you ready to order?!" I haven't quite reached the Private Godfrey from Dad's Army stage, though, so maybe there is hope for me yet!

As a direct result of all this progress we felt it would be possible for us to try to get a couple of days away as a sort of mini-holiday, so we actually did manage to book a short break at a hotel in Southport in August. We timed it to coincide with the opening day of the Southport Flower Show and chose a hotel that wasn't far away from where it was being held. Ian took us and deposited us at the hotel, and it turned out to be a resounding success. We were blessed with good weather throughout most of the time when we were outdoors, and I didn't have too much difficulty within the hotel as our room was on the ground floor as were all of the other amenities we needed during our stay – dining-room, bar, I didn't need anything else!

We went for a walk along the prom during the afternoon we arrived, Su pushing me in the wheelchair part of the way, then me using the crutches, and it all went very well. We used the same process the following day at the Flower Show and it worked a treat. I had never been to the Flower Show before, but Su has enjoyed going there on a number of occasions and I felt it was time that she should be able to get full benefit from our short break – and she did!

Ian and Eileen picked us up from the hotel the next day and we spent an hour or two bird-watching at Marshside, on the coast road just on the edge of the town, before they took us to a café in Astley Park in Chorley for afternoon tea! All in all it rounded off a most enjoyable few days and pointed the way to what we may possibly be able to manage in the future.

A couple of old friends of mine, John and Glennis, were kind enough to get in touch and invite me to join them to watch a couple of local cricket matches on the two Bank Holidays in May, and the second of those became the springboard for the publicity which has come my way since, and ultimately gave me the idea and opportunity to write this and attempt to launch the fund.

The editor of the local paper, the Chorley Guardian, Chris Maguire, happened to be at the game and I had known him from a few years earlier when I had done some football reports for him. He hadn't heard what had happened to me in the intervening couple of years, and was clearly interested, and also as a true journalist he sensed the idea of a story! Before I knew it there I was gracing the pages of the aforementioned Chorley Guardian. Everything else just snowballed from there – Chorley F.C., my lifelong passion, had appointed a high-profile manager in ex-Manchester City and Blackburn Rovers midfielder Garry Flitcroft, and before I knew what was happening Chris had secretly arranged with Su that they would spring a surprise on me by calling round unexpectedly. Garry presented me with a replica shirt with my name on it and they invited me to Chorley's annual pre-season fixture against Preston North End. This is a match which has taken place every year in memory of Jack Kirkland, an ex-Chorley chairman since his death in 2003, and I was asked if I would present the cup for which it is played to the winning captain. Obviously I agreed and was chauffeured to the game with Christopher in a Bentley no less! The only downside was that I had to hand the cup to the Preston captain, and not to Chorley's, but that was hardly a surprise as they have won it every year since its inception!

More publicity has followed that at intervals, and Chris keeps in touch from time to time to see how I'm getting on, though his contact with me nowadays is more personal than professional as he has moved on to pastures new in his work. I've been able to attend a number of matches since then, thanks to my team of chauffeurs, for whom I should give honourable mention – my nephew David (Bob's eldest), our Christopher and fellow long-term Chorley follower John Wells. They are usually accompanied by Bill Yates, another staunch supporter over many years who has also filled most roles at the club at one time or another – caretaker manager, assistant manager, reserves manager, etc. etc. To that list now can be added disabled wheelchair pusher! With all the practice they get between them things usually go smoothly, for home matches anyway! Away is a different story as we invariably get lost and as I am new to this disability game you never quite know what to expect when you get there, so every trip is like a new adventure!

By November I was even able to get to a 'gig' as Christopher and I went to see Status Quo at the Guild Hall in Preston, and that was followed in 2011 by a number of comedy shows, Milton Jones at the Lowry in Salford, Phil Cool at the Little Theatre in Chorley and in summer at the same venue ventriloquist Paul Zerdin. Rachael bought her mum and dad tickets to see Strictly Come Dancing on Tour in Liverpool a few weeks ago and Christopher provided us with a taxi service for what turned out to be another memorable evening. Add trips to the cinema to see The King's Speech and The Best Exotic Marigold Hotel and a number of meals at various pubs and restaurants and you can see that since my arrival home there has been a slow but steady improvement in my condition to the extent that I am now able to do a number of things which I could only have dreamt about in the dark days of 2009. But there was one single event in 2010 which overshadowed everything else and gave me the largest boost on recuperation road...

Chapter 9

Charlie!

The biggest possible aid to my recovery arrived on May 18th 2010 – our first grandson Charlie! What a delight he has been right from the off! Christopher and Alison have been very good in ensuring that we are able to see him as often as possible. His very presence here is a real tonic for both Su and me and his happy smiling face creates such a positive atmosphere in complete contrast to how things were a couple of years ago.

Every time we see him he seems to be making progress and it's a joy to see him developing in such a positive way. Far from my dread that the very idea of a grandchild would put years on me, if anything it's rejuvenated us both, although my physical limitations mean that I can't be quite as active with him as I would like to be. The bigger he gets, too, the more difficult that will be, I suspect, but even just watching him play and learn as he goes along is wonderful!

I thought it would be nice for him to have a whole chapter to himself so that if the worst came to the worst and he never gets to know me properly he would at least be aware that I knew him and he would get a little insight as to how much he has meant to his grandad. If that sounds like a very pessimistic scenario of the future then I should add that I dearly hope it doesn't turn out like that but if it does then I think it's a nice little legacy for him.

Chapter 10

Checkups!

C harlie has had that full chapter all to himself, now it's the turn of my routine checkups to take centre stage, because checkup days are different from any other. I can make light of most other days, but not those when I have to go for a checkup. They are sombre days indeed, or that's how they start off...

The anxieties begin in the days leading up to the checkup.It starts with me having to have a blood test a week or two in advance, not my favourite procedure but one which I have managed to get used to since my days in hospital when I had one almost every other day. I feel reluctant to make any arrangements for the future during those days leading up to the checkup in case the results tell me there isn't going to be much of a future, but I am the first to admit that you can't live your life that way or you'd never do anything. So if something is arranged which is timed later than my checkup day I push it to the back of my mind in case it turns out that I won't be able to go through with it. For a short period of time the checkup is the focal point of my total existence.

The night before is quite a nervy time once I've got to bed. Sleep doesn't come quite as easily as it usually does as the doubts play havoc with any composure I may have been able to pretend I had up to that point. Eventually I do slumber but it seems to be in fits and starts until it's time to get up, only then do I feel I could fall into a really deep sleep – but that's a pleasure which on these occasions is denied me.

On the actual day everything is wrong from the outset. Most of my days only really begin towards other people's lunchtime as I can normally only last a maximum of twelve hours and I prefer to have the longer time in the evening rather than the morning! But on these sent-from-hell days I'm expected to be ready for when my patient transport is due, i.e. an hour before my appointment. Not that that is a guarantee that they will arrive on time but I have to be ready in case they are. If that sounds ungrateful, I'm not really, quite the contrary in fact, but if I'm trying to build up the drama of checkup days, I really have to don the mantle of a genuine Mr.Grumpy, haven't I?

I never want anything to eat when I get up on these mornings but Su says I have to – so I do! Once upon a time I wouldn't have been able to swallow anything, my nerves being so tight, but I seem to be able to manage nowadays so it shows I must have improved a little, doesn't it?

Then we sit and wait (and wait and wait – but that's really a couple of waits too many to be honest, because in truth they are usually quite prompt!), then we go through the motions of forced cheerfulness with comments about the weather and such before going on the journey in almost complete silence, often having to pick up other patients en route, and the stilted conversation resumes again briefly till the demand for such niceties has been satisfied, then I sink back into my morbid reverie, my thoughts dominated by worrying what the outcome of my checkup might be. I seem to just talk incessantly to myself. None of it makes much sense so it's perhaps as well it's only for my own inner ears. These checkups really are a matter of life and death, or at least it seems that way, even though the worst scenario isn't likely to be quite as extreme as that. It could be that I may have to embark on a new course of treatment which may or may not involve more stays in hospital. For me, though, it isn't necessarily the thought of what specifically might happen, but just the idea that after having had such a good run this could be the start of the downward spiral towards, well, I think you know where this is going, don't you? Contrast that with getting a favourable result and you should be able to understand the conflict of emotions which envelops me on these mornings. It brings back memories of waiting for exam results, and I possibly have some idea what X-Factor and Strictly Come Dancing finalists are going through at "the moment of truth", but the consequences are rather more far-reaching for me, wouldn't you agree?

So we arrive at the hospital and have a long trek, or to be more accurate Su has a long trek as I am in a wheelchair being pushed by her, and eventually we reach the clinic. Anyone who has ever had an appointment at a clinic knows that appointment times don't really mean what they say, and you might as well go there being prepared to camp out as you are almost certainly destined to have a long wait before you eventually get summoned. I can never concentrate on anything while I'm waiting so I just sit there with the same thoughts that have been with me since I woke up going round and round in my mind over and over again. By the time I'm called I'm convinced it's going to be bad news even though up to now it never has been so five minutes later I feel ready to dance and sing my way back home! The relief is enormous – it may only be three or four months grace until the next time, but for me it is all the foreseeable future.

The contrast between the journey there and the return one is stark, though doubtless wouldn't be should the result of the checkup not be a favourable one. All the tentative arrangements which have been pushed to the back of my mind can now be confirmed, future events which I have been reluctant to dwell on can now be keenly anticipated, in short my life which has been kept on hold for a few days can now be resumed – at least until the next checkup is due...!

Chapter 11

The Present...

If you've managed to get so far in the narrative, well done, not much further to go now, but I hope you're not feeling sorry for me. I may be living on borrowed time, but who isn't? Any bookie giving survival odds would maybe not give me any favourable figures at lasting too long, but they do get things wrong occasionally, don't they?

Consider, then, my life as it is and perhaps you may end up wishing you had such a cushy existence! I've never been a good'un at getting up in the morning but the dictates of being a working man always meant that I had to be out of bed at a certain time every day, so I did, and got whatever lie-ins I could at the weekend. I had always thought that when I retired I would probably get a lie-in most mornings, but I know that Su would never have let these be long ones. However, as it turns out, I get a lie-in every day unless I have to get up for one of those dreaded hospital checkups or if it's one of those rare occasions when we've got something arranged which necessitates an early start.

So, I make sure I am at least up at the crack of noon! For those of you in that club which says that when you do that you miss the best part of the day I should point out that the nature of my illness dictates that I can only stay up for a limited time and whereas one would tend to think that a normal day consists of about sixteen hours, for me it's nearer to twelve and I like to stay up till fairly late at night so I make up for that by staying in bed in the morning. It was originally suggested that I could split my day by having a nap in the afternoon but that's never been something I've ever wanted to do. I tried it a couple of times in the early days after I came home and found that if I did have a lie-down in the afternoon I either couldn't get to sleep or, if I did, I didn't then want to get up and that defeated the objective somewhat so we've reached this compromise – I get up late morning and stay up as long as I either want or am able to. Yet another reason why I am reluctant to get up is that I am always comfortable in bed in the morning, and I know that when I do get up a decidedly uncomfortable ordeal awaits me in the form of the morning ablutions and getting dressed.

I have my first pills of the day as soon as I wake up for the first time, usually between eight- and nine-o'clock as that's round about the time Su gets up. These have to be taken an hour before I eat so I know that that's fairly safe! The next time I wake up, normally between ten and eleven, I have my second lot of pills, painkillers, hopefully to prepare me for when I do take the plunge.

Once I've made the decision to get up I have to do my first exercise of the day, raising each leg into the air in turn till I've done twenty, then I immediately sit on the edge of the bed and hoist myself up before hobbling to the bathroom. Having arrived at the sanctuary of the bathroom,

I plonk myself on the loo for at least five minutes if for no other reason on occasions than to get my breath back. My wash then usually takes a further ten minutes before I slowly venture back to the bedroom to get dressed. These days I can manage the whole procedure of getting my clothes on without human assistance, though I wouldn't be able to get my socks on without the help of the aptly-named sock-aid. This is only a piece of plastic with some shoelace-type string attached, but is quite ingenious how it works merely by putting the sock onto the plastic, inserting the foot into the sock while it's still round the plastic, then pulling the plastic out using the aforementioned string and, voila, the operation is complete, sock in place! Right, now the other one…

By the time I've got myself downstairs I'm usually quite exhausted so I sit in my recliner while I recover and start on one of my main jobs of the day – reading the Radio Times to see what we might want to watch or record that day. While doing that I have my brunch, fruit juice and cereals. By the time that's out of the way I'm usually fully recovered and ready to switch on my laptop to start work (such as what I do on the laptop constitutes being called 'work'!) but before I do that I must do the rest of my exercises! These were given to me by the last physio who called to see me and all have to be done standing, apart from the ones which I do before I get up. So I stand at the fireplace in the lounge or work surface in the kitchen using them to hold on to as I start with my Harry Worth impression! For those of you not old enough to remember how he used to start his television show all those years ago, just google "Harry Worth window" and watch it on youtube. Well I've got ten of those to do with each leg, then ten with each knee raised up as high as I can get it (not far, I fear!), ten with each leg stretched behind me in turn and, to finish with, ten standing on my toes and ten with my heels raised off the ground. Once they're finished I limp over to the wall and bend down to plug in the laptop, then make my way back to my recliner and I'm finally ready to start.

First things first, a game of Freecell while everything else is being opened up. When in doubt, or if I want a break from what I'm doing, Freecell is usually my first port of call! I wouldn't say I'm addicted to it, but I'm sure Su would! Having said that, though, while I was in hospital I had no laptop with me and Su tried to persuade me to let her bring it in, and she used Freecell as the carrot dangled in front of me feeling certain that it would persuade me, but at that stage it didn't. As a result, when I went to Cuerden Grange and was reunited with my laptop, I had forgotten how to play it and had to learn it from scratch all over again. If you aren't familiar with it, it's not really important that you know anything about it, other than that it's a card game of patience which you play on a computer, and as it is believed that every game is winnable, that is my challenge, and I won't let a game go until I have won it. In that sense it is addictive, I suppose, but there could be worse things to which one could be overly attached – aren't there?! It's playing this game which leaves me in no doubt that I am the son of my father, for he seemed to spend most of his leisure time playing conventional games of patience, hour after hour, day after day, though it wasn't all he did in his spare time. He did also enjoy reading crime novels and a reasonable amount of television watching. When I questioned him about the patience he said that he'd always enjoyed card games but had seen so many friendships come to an end as a result that he'd decided patience was the best game to play as the only person you would be likely to fall out with would be yourself!.

Emails are my next task once that first Freecell is done, and there's usually an odd message or two waiting for me. Very often these are the usual round of 'funnies' sent as a rule but not always by either Christopher or Alan, but often there will be messages which need attending to or where replies are warranted, so I deal with those before doing a bit of surfing on the Internet. While the potential sources of the 'net are vast, in practice I only visit a relatively small number of sites, but the ones I do use I go to regularly (no, none of them are 'those' kind of sites!). I do quite a bit of browsing on ebay, mainly looking for football programmes to fill in gaps in my collection.

I've spent a lot of time continuing something which I started before I was ill too, and this is all centred around my itunes library. I've managed to put all our CDs on there, and I've bought quite a number of tracks either from the itunes store or from Amazon, but the major work has been the retrospective conversion of my old vinyl and tape collection. Su has bought me the appropriate machines for this purpose as Christmas or birthday presents and I've just about completed it now, as a result of which I now have an itunes library comprising in excess of 9,000 tracks!

I've always been fond of pop music ever since Bob introduced me to it as a young lad, though my tastes are considerably wider now than they were back in the late fifties. But how often have you stood in front of your record collection and not known what you want to listen to? It's always been a dream of mine, long before it was technically possible to do so, to have all my albums and singles in one place so I could switch a machine on and just play songs from my collection in any random order, and that's what I am able to do now with my ipod – absolutely brilliant!

The rest of my time on the laptop is spent writing, either this, which is predominant at the moment, or the articles I write for the football programme, or anything else that might take my fancy.

Some afternoons I break off part way through to go for a walk, usually to accompany Su when she's off to do a bit of shopping. Early on I only used to go part of the way with her, and you can read into that what you will (if you must!), but once I got carried away and ended up in the supermarket with her! That was quite an eventful outing as I got myself registered to use one of their scooters and went up and down the aisles on that. Since then it's become more often than not that I make the full journey with her, a round trip of almost a mile.

Alan also comes to visit once a week (when he's not on holiday, which is considerably more often than most people are!) and usually takes me for a ride in his top down (weather permitting!) sporty car "chasing lassies" – his phrase, not mine, though I'm sure that nowadays like me he'd run a mile if he ever caught one! It doesn't stop him pretending though and has resulted in me giving him the title "playboy of the Western world"!

When I think about Alan I wonder whether he should be the one writing about events in his life rather than his younger brother. Bob, Barbara and I have all being married around forty years and so has Alan, though with the slight difference that his grand total has been amassed with three different wives! We've all said that we think he must be partial to wedding cake, but he denies that that has anything to do with it. He's also had his share of problems over the years, mainly due to an addiction to alcohol which I think he blames at least partially on previously unhappy marriages. We never suspected anything at the time – yes, we knew he liked a drink as we all did, but he carried it to extremes, but in secret. To illustrate how successfully secretive he was, even Sylvia, his wife, knew nothing about it! The first we knew was when she rang to tell us that he'd been admitted to the Priory. It's been wonderful, though, to see how he's turned his life around to the extent that not only has he not had an alcoholic drink for ten years now but also he has got to the stage where he helps others who are experiencing the same problems he had. He's always been one to do whatever he does to extremes, probably the reason why he's had the rollercoaster existence which he has had, so it follows that when he decided to become a blood donor he didn't just give the odd pint every now and then, or waited to be invited – no, he goes out looking to see where he can donate his next one! As a result he's racked up a massive eighty pints up to now, and still counting. He tells me that all this is his way of making up for past wrongdoings, and this is also why he sponsors a child in Africa, and he is clearly very proud of the way his young protégé writes to him and sends him photos so that he can keep an eye on his progress. As he's never had any children of his own I think he finds this a rewarding substitute. So when people start looking for heroes I think Alan should be much nearer the front of the queue than I could ever have been.

And speaking of heroes, before he was ill Ian was another regular caller, and he took Su and me to do a bit of bird-watching on another occasion apart from the visit to Marshside when we had been staying in Southport, this time at Mere Sands Wood. This was a regular place where Su and I enjoyed many an afternoon before my illness, twitching having become one of our hobbies in recent years. Ian could always be relied on as well to give me lifts to the library so that I could catch up with my friends there.

His illness has meant that that has had to be put on hold for the time being, but it's possibly given me the opportunity to aim for something else in the future. I hadn't used any public transport since becoming wheelchair-bound but Ian's enforced absence encouraged me to attempt to rectify that? After all, Su and I have both got our bus passes now! So, with no little trepidation, we ventured into town to do a bit of shopping and as that had been successful we thought it would be a good idea to try to use the same mode of transport the next time I was due to have a library visit. So now, having succeeded with that little venture, as Arfur Daley used to say, "the world's our lobster"! Who knows where our adventures might take us in the future...?!!?

And I can now answer that question because between writing that last paragraph and starting this one Su and I have been to Amsterdam! Spurred on by the progress I have managed this year I took the plunge and surprised Su by booking an Easter weekend mini-cruise. We were picked up by coach locally on Good Friday and taken to Hull where we took the overnight ferry to Rotterdam, or to be more accurate the ferry took us!

The coach took us into Amsterdam on Saturday morning after breakfast and even though we had to put up with a traffic holdup for about twenty minutes, christened a 'Rotter-jam' by someone on the coach, we arrived at our destination around 11o'clock and spent the next six hours dodging pedestrians, trams, buses, the occasional car but mainly bikes, more bikes and yet more bikes, and all in what you might call very warm weather! It wasn't just Su and I who were exhausted by the time we got back on the coach, which is possibly not surprising as I suspect there were only a handful of the other 33 passengers on the trip who were younger than us! I may have been the only one with a wheelchair but many of the others seemed to have joints which were creaking even more than mine were!

Because of how busy it was, we weren't able to go into any shops or museums with having to take the wheelchair and crutches everywhere with us. As a result we hardly spent any of the euros which we'd taken with us, except for the 50 cents which I'd had to pay for use of the conveniences on the Central Station! 50 cents for 1p – I didn't think much of that conversion rate, I don't mind telling you!

Back to the ferry then and all its facilities before arriving back in Hull early on Easter Sunday morning and back home at lunchtime. It was an enjoyable if tiring couple of days, not unexpectedly, and has certainly opened up the way for us to attempt other trips. Speaking of which, we have also been on an enjoyable four-day visit to the Cotswolds, one of our favourite areas in the country and one where I spent two years at college as a teenager, so that's been another successful venture for us. The only drawback was the weather during one of our excursions when the rain was so bad that we decided to stay on the coach rather than risk another soaking and we renamed the village where we were as Bourton-under-Water! Despite that the mini-break as a whole was deemed another success.

And then there's Charlie! If it's a day when he's coming, forget everything else, he takes priority for our attention, and rightly so – but of course you'll have gathered that from the earlier chapter which bore his name!

If I'm at home at four o'clock it's my job to make us a brew and possibly have a biscuit or piece of cake. This is obviously a small thing in itself, but an important part of my progress. I could never have envisaged being able to do everything that constitutes making a drink while lying in that hospital bed. Muscles that hadn't been used for over a year had to be roused from their slumber. All the different exercises and small tasks which I do in the course of a day, though doubtless considerably less than most people do anyway in the course of their day, must of their very nature be beneficial for me, or I wouldn't put myself through them if I felt that wasn't the case.

My 'working' day comes to an end about 6.30 which is the time when we usually have our evening meal – I bet you wish your working day was as short and easy as mine, don't you?! The rest of the day then is spent watching the box, either 'live' TV or something we've recorded, or one of the many DVDs we own or have on rare occasions borrowed from the library. I don't tend to use the library service too much now that I've left and my visits there are mainly for social reasons.. I've already said that I'm not much of a reader and the only book I've borrowed in the last three years was a guidebook to Amsterdam just before we went there. I'm more interested in the CDs and DVDs that they stock, but despite the fact that I worked for the service for forty-three years, I no longer have any of the privileges which I enjoyed while I was on the staff, so strictly speaking I should have to pay to borrow any of these. It is a source of great resentment to me, that once you've left everything you've done seems to be forgotten and there is no borrower category allowing us in our latter years to continue to enjoy free use of their facilities. In practical terms it doesn't cause me any great hardship, and because I still have many friends working in the libraries I visit, they are inclined to waive any charges, but they shouldn't have to do that in my opinion, and it's the principle which I strongly resent. You may well not agree with me, especially in these days of cutbacks, but if you knew only half of how much public money gets wasted, you'd be appalled, I'm sure. For example, you will appreciate that in order to keep library stocks up-to-date new books are purchased regularly but of course older and less popular ones have then to be removed to make room for the new ones, but have you ever wondered what happens to these? If managers would only take the decision to try and recoup some of their outlay by selling them and recycling what they can't sell, I'm sure they could easily finance a system whereby us 'oldies' could be allowed to continue free use of the service as a small thankyou for long service, and I reckon they'd still have thousands left for other projects.. Right, I guess I've burned my bridges now, not much chance of them buying copies of this for their shelves, I don't suppose! Not to worry, at least I've got it off my chest now and it is something about which I felt strongly long before it was my turn to retire.

I've mentioned earlier that now I'm able to go out as well, it is open for us to go to the cinema or a pub/restaurant if we want as an alternative, which we have done quite a few times now. One of our favourite places which is only just over a mile away so not too expensive taxi-wise is called the Hospital Inn, and believe me their hospital food is a whole lot better than I received in Royal Preston!

I've been taken to a few leaving 'dos' for some of my former work colleagues as well, and I have also managed to get to a number of football matches, not just the Saturday afternoons but some evening games too, so my disability isn't turning out to be quite as restricting as I'd feared it might have been, thank goodness.

Unfortunately I have also had to attend a couple of funerals of ex-work colleagues, both of whom were diagnosed with cancer a long time after I was, yet they have both succumbed to it before me. It's very sad, especially when I think that one of them was amongst my visitors while I was in hospital and at Cuerden, and neither of us would ever have thought for one moment that I would outlive him.

And then it's bedtime! As in the morning I tend to be somewhat reluctant to embark on this ritual, because it is a distinctly uncomfortable procedure, so I often delay it for a while. When I was first able to sit in the lounge and watch television with Su I used to go to bed immediately after the national and local news about 10.30 but it's nearly always after 11 these days, and even later at weekends if I'm watching Match Of The Day!

Eventually I get there and I'm allowed to have my supper in bed (unless I've stopped up later than my beloved!), and I have to have an injection in my tum every night too, so she kindly administers that to me. It's something which I would have dreaded once upon a time but it really is no big deal now that I'm used to it, though I'm glad that Su is prepared to do it as I still don't think I could bear to do it to myself. I reckoned up once and I think she's given me almost 1000 jabs so far – and still counting! What would I do without her…?!

I have a read after supper then lie down and listen to my ipod until I drift off into the land of nod – night-night, zzzzzzzzzzzzz!

Chapter 12

Wedding Bells!

C hristopher and Alison had decided that they wanted to get married some time ago, and they probably would have done long before Charlie's arrival had it not been for my illness. They had talked about it to us back in 2008 with the likelihood that they would have gone ahead with it the following year had I not put a spanner in the works – I don't know, I always seem to get the blame for everything!

Once I was back home and clearly making good progress they decided it was time to broach the subject again. I'm sure they would have got married whether they had our blessing or not, but that was never likely to arise as we were more than happy to see them tie the knot. They only wanted it to be a small 'do', with invitations going to immediate family and a few close friends only, and they said that they would like to do all the arranging themselves. We did offer to help out financially, as did Alison's parents, but they remained keen to pay for all the main elements themselves, but eventually agreed to let both sets of parents make contributions to cover some of the fringe expenditure.

So the date was set for the afternoon of Thursday August 11th at Rochdale Town Hall followed by a reception at the very highly rated Nutters Restaurant just a couple of miles away. It turned out to be a wonderful day, but of course with it being us there inevitably had to be a few obstacles to be overcome along the way.

With only a week to go before the wedding Su was suddenly taken ill with severe stomach pains, resulting in me insisting that we send for the doctor. Fortunately the medication supplied by him did the trick sand she was soon back on her feet, but the episode brought home to us just how dependent we are on her maintaining good health. I did what I could but felt a bit useless – I couldn't even look after myself for any length of time, let alone care for a sick wife as well. Rachael did offer to stay at home but as she is in a job where she doesn't get paid if she doesn't go into work we were reluctant to let her do that. She was sufficiently worried about us that she came home at lunchtime anyway, just after the doctor had gone and in time to take Su's prescription to the chemist's.

Then it was my turn! The very day before the nuptials I had a recurrence of the mouth problem which had afflicted me for a few weeks earlier in the year and which had only been in abeyance for about a fortnight. That was quite a blow as it meant that not only was eating difficult, but so was conversation. Fortunately I wasn't going to have to make a speech, that would have been nigh on impossible, but a social occasion such as this would of necessity involve a lot of small talk and this was likely to be a difficult proposition. As it turned out, while I was considerably less loquacious than usual, maybe that was for the better and once I had imbibed one or two alcoholic beverages the pain was certainly less prominent. I managed to eat as well which was very fortunate as the fare on offer was outstanding and many were heard to say that it was the best meal they had ever had at a wedding – praise indeed, and well merited.

The only downside of a memorable day was the weather – windy and wet, it meant that outside photographs were kept to a minimum, and we weren't able to take advantage of the lovely grounds in which Nutters is situated. Other than that it was a most enjoyable and memorable day for all of us, and yet another occasion which I couldn't have dared to hope I would be able to go to a couple of years ago.

Chapter 13 (or 12a for the superstitious!)
… & The Future…?

I f you think I've painted a rosy picture of my current situation, that has been deliberate, but obviously that isn't the whole story. I've described the stress and tension which surround my checkup days, but those aren't the only hospital visits I've had since I came home as I have also had to go for other treatments. These took place early in the year after my return home and gave us a few trips to the seaside in Blackpool.

It was felt that I might be able to benefit at some stage in the future by undergoing a bone marrow transplant of sorts. As my cancer has been in remission, I was told that they should be able to harvest some of my healthy stem cells and then either transplant them as part of the same procedure or put them into storage for some time in the future. I was initially somewhat reluctant to undergo any further treatment while conceding that I knew it was all only being suggested for my own good. Having spent a full year away from home, and feeling relatively well now, I really didn't want to upset the applecart in any way, and part of the information I was given left me in no doubt that the second part of the treatment would mean having to spend a few more weeks in hospital, and as it would have a severe impact on my immune system would probably leave me feeling quite unwell for some time. In the end the specialist and I decided on a compromise – I would have the cells harvested but not have them put back until and unless they were needed and, in a nutshell, that is what took place. The actual procedure didn't go through without the odd little problem along the way, and my blood pressure fell to an extent that it did cause some concern for a short time before settling down again, and at least it's done now and it's useful to know that these cells are there if/when needed, but it has meant that I haven't had to spend more than the odd day in hospital, and long may that continue!

It's possibly worth bearing in mind too that the days when I tend to do the bulk of my writing will inevitably be my good days. The days when I'm finding everything a bit of a struggle or not feeling particularly well will be the days when the last thing I want to be doing is writing, or for that matter indulging in anything but the essentials, so that possibly gives something of an imbalanced view.

Another unfortunate obstacle which hasn't yet been overcome concerns my eyesight. I have referred to another of my old friends, Phil, earlier in the narrative.and told you that he was also my optician. I was starting to get somewhat concerned about a deterioration in my eyesight while at Cuerden so once I was back home he gave me a thorough test. It didn't take him long to realise that I had got cataracts, probably as a result of the drugs I'd been on for my chemotherapy. Needless to say I wasn't too enamoured by his verdict, although not greatly surprised as it was clear to me that everything was far from as it should be in that department. He reckoned he could do something for me in the short term for one of my eyes at least and there was a distinct improvement when he supplied me with some new spectacles, but that unfortunately didn't last more than a few months and it's become quite limited yet again to the extent that I have now almost completely lost the sight in my right eye apart from being able to make out bits of colour, or light and shade.

It is of course possible for me to get this problem sorted with another trip to the hospital and Su is very keen that I should do so while the rest of me is bearing up quite well. She's quite anxious that were my condition to take a downturn better eyesight than I have currently got would be an absolute must and naturally I take her point. My lack of cooperation comes partly from me reverting to type and avoiding anything to do with hospitals unless absolutely necessary and partly because I am reluctant to do anything which might adversely affect my current positive state. The potential advantages are enormous, I do appreciate that, and it's not out of the question to think that it might even be possible for me to resume driving were I to get it sorted. But what if it wasn't successful? Where would that leave me? It may be that I do have to sit quite close to the TV to watch it but at least I can do that, it doesn't bear thinking about not having any sight at all.

I have to confess also that there is still a fair amount of pain to be endured every day. I've said before that it would be easier for me to stay in bed and do nothing but what sort of existence would that be? Far better to grin and bear it as far as possible, so that's what I do. The pain isn't incessant and I often bring to mind the story of the chap who kept banging his head against a wall. When asked why he did it he said, "Because it feels so good when I stop!" In the same way I know that once I've managed to get up in the morning and am washed and dressed, then struggled my way downstairs to the haven of my reclining chair, within five minutes the pain has eased and I'm ready to move on and face the rest of the day.

The same applies when I get out of my chair to do my exercises or go out for a walk, it's painful to begin with but it eases and I feel the benefit later. I've often been asked what form this pain takes and the nearest I can get to describing it is to imagine someone's got a piece of fine sandpaper, and they are gently sanding you down – I realise that unless you are something of a masochist it probably doesn't happen to you very often but try to visualise what it might feel like and you'll have some idea how it is for me. It's like a burning sensation and while it doesn't double me up with the intensity of it as a toothache, earache or headache might do, it is distinctly uncomfortable. As the area of this discomfort is more or less just where I had the shingles, it makes me think that it is a relic of that condition rather than to do with the myeloma. It does feel like I'm wearing a sandpaper belt, and when I go out I feel like a snail – that's not just because of the speed I travel, or lack of it, but also because it feels like I'm carrying my house on my back!

More recently too I've been suffering from neuralgia and toothache which isn't surprising as my phobia about all things medical had its most obvious outlet where dentists were concerned. Put it this way, I hadn't set foot inside any dentist's surgery for more than forty years! Of course that has presented me with myriad difficulties over the years but I've had to grin and bear it as that was a necessary consequence of embarking on such a stupid course of action, or lack of it. Nowadays, though, it's been harder to put up with in addition to my other medical problems so Su has insisted that I swallow my pride and go – so I did! The outcome of that was another couple of hospital visits in December where I had a total of six teeth taken out. I have to confess that like so many other things in this story it was nowhere near as bad an experience as I'd dreaded it might be but unfortunately the pain which had been the reason for my trips to the dentist and hospital didn't just go away as we'd hoped it would. This has meant more visits to the dentist's and she has deduced that the source of my problem is actually a wisdom tooth which is moving horizontally in my gum. The extractions have given it space to move but the dentist has said that she thinks it will settle down once my gums have fully healed up so we've agreed to leave it like that for now as the alternative would be yet another hospital trip and you must know by now how I'd feel about that! With a bit of luck too we hope that I'll be more sensible in the future and undergo regular checkups and accept whatever treatment may be necessary. Perhaps one day I may even be able to smile properly for any photographs for a change!

Dr.Kanyike usually asks me as part of my checkup if I suffer from bone pain and it may be that some of the pain that I've been getting more recently is that, though sometimes aches and pains can be difficult to describe and also on occasions to locate exactly where they are – or is that just me?!

There's also the additional worry that my immune system is probably still not as good as it might be, so I still have to be wary of simple things like colds. I have had a few since I came home but fortunately most of them haven't developed into anything worse, apart from one around the New Year just gone when I had to have a visit from the doctor who prescribed yet more antibiotics. Fortunately these seemed to do the trick for me and we live in hopes that the flu jab I had late last year will help to keep worse conditions at bay.

Having said all that negative stuff, and this chapter does seem so far to have been nothing but a catalogue of ailments, my condition overall is probably as good as it's ever likely to be. I've made an incredible amount of progress since I came home but we've reached a plateau now and I don't envisage much more improvement, but I would settle for a consolidation of what I've got if I can't make any more progress than I already have. I've no idea what the future might hold for me, but who does? If I said that I hope it's the myeloma that eventually sees me off, don't misunderstand me! I don't mean soon, but having spent the last three years learning how to live with it I'd be extremely peeved if a heart attack came along and suddenly knocked me into eternity! It just wouldn't seem right somehow!

At the start of the 2010/11 football season I decided to place a bet that Chorley would win the league. It isn't the first time I have placed this bet but I did feel that this time there were genuine reasons for us to believe that our optimism wouldn't be totally misplaced. As it's asking a lot to think that we might win it outright I decided to settle for an each-way bet. As we led the table for much of the early part of the season it looked like we might actually come out on top but eventually we only just managed to scrape 3rd place, but at least that was enough for me to come out of the transaction with a profit. My initial outlay had been £40 but I received £80 back, not a bad return on my investment. However, had we won the league I would have got £340 back, clearly considerably more than I did get. It would be easy for me to feel bitter about certain games in which we dropped points and think that we could or maybe even should have won the league. That would be wrong anyway as the two teams who finished above us did so because they deserved to, and in some ways 3rd place did flatter us. Despite this, I am nevertheless delighted to be able to say that not only did our third place give me a profit and my club a place in the playoffs, but we have actually won those playoffs to gain promotion, the first time we have done so since 1988!

I apologise for going on at some length about my team but the story of my bet and what I might have won compared to what I actually did win has a distinct parallel with my current life situation! Su and I are often asked how we view our life now, and people often appear surprised at our positive outlook. It would be easy for us to look at what we haven't got and feel bitter about it but what would be the point of that? We are fully aware that our retirement has not turned out as we had imagined or indeed hoped that it might be. But we almost had no retirement at all, at least not as a couple! So we are keen to stress that we are grateful that we have got what we have, and focus solely on that. Anything other than that would make us appear bitter and twisted, and we wouldn't like to be remembered like that, would we?!

In the meantime, though, I really do feel that I've got plenty of living left to do before I get a visit from Mr.G.Reaper. I'd like to see this published as an e-book to start with, then perhaps appear in hard copy too, and make some money for charity as a result. It would gladden my heart to see the first donations being handed over. Having said that, I have resisted one or two suggestions that have been put to me regarding ways we might supplement any donations given to us. In particular I didn't think it was a good idea to ask people to sponsor me for each day, week or month I manage to survive as has been suggested by one interested party! I quite easily envisaged becoming quite unpopular were I to last longer than prospective donors felt appropriate and I wouldn't really want anyone saying or thinking "and about time too!" once I do shake off this mortal coil!

But as to what I may do once the book has been completed and seen the light of day, who knows? Hopefully I may get some more writing done especially if we've succeeded in generating some interest with this little offering. Anything else is in God's hands – He's been good to me so far, but I'll gladly accept a bit more if He's offering...

Epilogue – Su's Story

Throughout all the time that the events contained in this book took place, I have been fully aware that it has only been giving you the picture from one viewpoint – mine! I have continually kept in mind, though, that Su must have been looking at everything that happened from a completely different perspective. As a result, once I'd finished most of my writing I invited her to read what I had done and asked her to consider adding anything of her own to supplement mine and illustrate her side of the story. What follows is the result and it's possibly fair to say that I have found her section as eye-opening as I think she found mine! It also shows that I am able to do what every husband who knows what's good for him does – always let your other half have the last word! You know it makes sense! Right, over to you, dear…

When I arrived home from hospital on the evening of John's admission I said to Christopher, "Life will never be the same again" How true, but little did I know then just what a rollercoaster of a ride it was going to be. For a start how on earth was my poor dear John going to cope with all this? A lifetime of being terrified of blood, hospitals, surgical operations and if needles were mentioned, the very likelihood was that he would pass out! The original diagnosis of this tumour being a secondary cancer with possibly worse news to follow of a primary somewhere was devastating. The thought that he might not walk again, information which was given to me, on my own, in Sister's office earlier that evening by the doctor who had accompanied us to the MRI suite and stayed until the scan was completed was just unthinkable.

John received this awful news with little expression on his face. Unfortunately the doctor who dropped the bombshell, someone we hadn't seen before, had decided to start offloading this information before Christopher and I had time to reach his bedside. I had been tearful when Christopher arrived and I'd had little time to compose myself before seeing John. Initially there were few words exchanged after the doctor left us. I knew that John would go into his shell and wouldn't want to talk about it. We all had our own thoughts but at least John's exclamation of "it's a bugger, this" and "sense of tumour" comment lightened the moment. I didn't want to leave him and return home but we were all very tired. It had been one hell of a day.

I sat at home on New Year's Eve constantly in touch with the hospital for news. I phoned every hour but was usually told that he was not yet back from theatre. This was followed by multiple text messages to others needing information. At 8.30pm I was told that he was in the recovery room and all was as well as could be expected. What a relief! Plenty more text messages were sent that night! A friend of mine came round to keep me company and I insisted that Rachael go out and celebrate the New Year as originally planned with her boyfriend.

John was in a side room when we visited on New Year's Day. I remember having to put on a plastic apron to prevent cross infection before we could enter the room. Strange times were to follow immediately after the operation. John kept all his visitors amused with his weird and wonderful stories, most of them under the influence of morphine of course!

A couple of days after John's operation I arranged a meeting with Mr Ray, the consultant who had carried out his operation. I went armed with a list of questions and my sister came with me not only for support but because two heads are definitely better than one in this sort of situation. We were told that his thoracic spine had become compressed at the level of the T9 vertebrae so a laminectomy was performed to decompress the spine and remove the tumour. Unfortunately the surgeons had not been able to remove all of the tumour because at some stage he'd started to bleed and to continue was too risky and would put his life in danger. We were also told that other areas of his spine were affected. The bone looked different on the MRI scan but not collapsed. Metal rods and plates were put in place to stabilise and strengthen the spine. We were shown the x rays of his spine with all this scaffolding. Amazing! He would be started on blood thinning injections and be referred to the Oncologist for radiotherapy and/ or chemotherapy. Their aim was to preserve the mobility that he had. All this information was hard to digest and I was so glad that my sister had taken notes so we had something to refer back to. It's fair to say that I was concerned that not all of the tumour had been removed and the obvious implications of this. He would at some stage be transferred to the oncology ward so there was no sign of a return home in the very near future.

When the accurate diagnosis of myeloma was given to us I felt that maybe he had been thrown a lifeline. I hadn't heard of it but treatable although not curable sounded a better option than the original diagnosis. Christopher went into overdrive and printed off masses of information about the illness from the Myeloma UK website. It was comforting to know that there was so much good information out there and I found this site invaluable then and still do.

The chemotherapy made John tired on some days and unexpectedly emotional on others. At least I always put the latter down to the tablets. I know he wasn't feeling sorry for himself and was remaining in remarkably good spirits. The old Blackburn humour was ever present! Nevertheless, on several occasions I received text messages from him suggesting that I came in to visit him on my own at first and I remember well the day that he had a towel covering his face as I approached his bed. He was sobbing beneath it. Up until then I could count on the fingers of one hand the number of times I'd seen my husband cry.

Towards the end of February, following a chat with one of John's physiotherapists I was distressed to discover that as he had made little significant physical progress so far it seemed unlikely that his condition was going to change. I should be thinking about how we would cope and manage his care if he returned home. I felt numb. How do you cope? Here is a man who has to be hoisted out of bed and can only sit relatively comfortably in a chair for about an hour per day. It was decided that a home visit by a community liaison officer should take place to assess the possibility of John returning home. Amazingly there was just enough room in the dining area of our dining kitchen for a hospital bed plus the compressor to run the air mattress which would hang at the end of the bed. Where would a hoist be stored? Well, in the kitchen of course! Every modern kitchen should have one. Obviously this was a non-starter because there would also be many other pieces of equipment needed near his bedside and who can, or would want to, live in a kitchen for 23 hours a day! A multi-disciplinary team meeting with social worker, specialist nurse, community liaison officer, physiotherapist, occupational therapist and me was arranged for 10th March. The social worker came up with the idea of John going into temporary residential care until we could investigate the possibility of an extension to the house. I said, "Don't tell him that!" but of course she had to. I found the conversations between the two of us regarding this move quite emotional but I had to keep it together for John's sake. All he wanted to do was come home.

Time marched on and my daily visits to the hospital became quite routine and I'm sure the bus drivers began to recognise me! Life was very surreal and continued to be so until John eventually came home. Even then, with a hospital bed in the dining room, all manner of equipment to help him get about and carers visiting nothing was back to any kind of normality.

While John was away it was my good fortune that I was able to sleep quite well. Of course come bedtime I was tired but that doesn't always bring sleep. Most mornings when I woke up I held a one-way conversation to whoever might be listening up there. This wasn't a prayer but a gentle request to watch over us. Then I'd throw back the duvet with a "let's get this show on the road" followed usually by the words 'onwards and upwards!' Alan frequently used to tell me to take it one day at a time. These are very wise words and I'm sure that along with the thoughts and prayers of family and friends this is what helped me to cope with whatever the day was to throw at me.

Unfortunately nothing prepared me for the phone call that I received from the hospital at 8.30a.m. on Wednesday 25th March 2009. "John's not well and his bloods are all over the place and we think that you should come in". "Are you telling me that this is serious?" I asked. "We think you should come in" was the reply. A quick phone call to Christopher ensured that we went to the hospital and dealt with this together. What on earth could have happened between me leaving John in good spirits and with no unusual symptoms at 8.30p.m. the previous evening and 8.30a.m. this morning? Well, pneumonia and septic shock actually! It is painful to revisit that day. The doctors were struggling to maintain his blood pressure and his breathing was giving cause for concern. We were told that he could go into respiratory failure and heart failure. The severity of the situation was obvious and I decided that Rachael and Barbara should be contacted. Poor Rachael. I waited outside the ward for her to arrive from work and unfortunately she thought the worst on seeing me there. Barbara's husband Ray was there to support her and Alison came to comfort Christopher and be there for Rachael. We were a family feeling so much pain that it was almost unbearable but we had each other. Christopher and I had to make decisions on that day that no one should ever have to make.

When we weren't with John we were camped out in a visitors room on the ward. Christopher and I had meetings with at one point two consultant haematologists, the registrar on the ward and the specialist haematology nurse. When the consultant from intensive care said that he wouldn't ventilate him it was decided that he needed a CPAP (Continuous Positive Airway Pressure) machine to aid his breathing. This machine needs to be operated by a trained nurse and the only machine available was on the coronary ward, so off we all went in convoy, John attached to saline, blood and anti-biotic drips and oxygen mask. The CPAP machine is non-invasive ventilation given through a sealed full-face mask held on securely by two straps which fit around the head. Unfortunately it has a very drying effect so breaks in its use are necessary He struggled to cope with these breaks but I was left in no doubt by one of the ward sisters that he would have to be weaned off this machine soon as it was only a temporary solution. I gave him sips of fluid and liquid food supplement called Ensure through a straw on a regular basis by unclipping this mask. Slowly the time that he spent on this machine was reduced and more active chest physio was started.

Sadly, a few days after John's transfer to coronary care his brother Bob died. This was not unexpected but John had not been made aware just how ill Bob was. It was impossible to think that he could be given this news whilst he was so poorly himself. We agonised about what should be done but I decided that I should tell him on the day prior to Bob's funeral. That way at least he could be there in spirit and could reflect on life with his oldest brother and all the memories that they shared.

Just before John suffered the pneumonia I had a consultation with a physiotherapist about the worsening condition of my arthritic right hip. She wondered if steroid injections would be beneficial and so I was sent to see an orthopaedic surgeon at the hospital. He looked at the x-ray and said that only a total hip replacement would do. I wasn't surprised by this but couldn't see just how possible this would be given our current situation.

Soon John returned to Ribblesdale Ward via a short spell in one of the chest wards. After suffering a pleural effusion he had a chest drain inserted to remove the fluid that had built up. Over a litre – I was amazed! He was still on oxygen therapy and had started having regular nebulisers. It was impossible to conduct a conversation whilst this was taking place due to the noise coming from the machine!

My life seemed to revolve around hospital visiting. Any necessary work was done in the morning. The rest of the time was spent at the hospital and when I arrived home in the evening there were always phone calls to be made and received from well-wishers and friends needing an update on John's condition. It was like being on a slow-moving roundabout. Visiting hours varied depending on which ward John was in. In the break between afternoon and evening visiting I would sit in the main seating area in the hospital either 'people watching' or reading. I was also kept entertained on many occasions by the sight of mummy duck and her brood who had taken up residency in a little grassed area just off one of the gardens which could be seen from the main hospital corridor. There were twelve ducklings and watching their antics and their steady growth certainly put a smile on my face. On other occasions I would visit Booths across the road from the hospital. They have a nice little café and of course there was always some food shopping to be done!

I had arranged a visit from an architect to discuss a rear extension to the house. I explained the situation and he said that he would draw up some rough plans for consideration. Very soon after, the idea of John leaving hospital reared its head again. He actually seemed resigned to a move to a nursing home and we tried to push the positive aspects i.e. different food, own room and hopefully closer to home. I went to look at a couple of nursing homes with Christopher. It was hard to take in that this was the sort of place in which John would have to reside for however long it would take. Cuerden Grange was chosen, the up-side being that it was only half a mile away from home. I had this rosy idea of visiting in the afternoon, home for tea and then back again early evening. My hip had other ideas! By this time I was walking with the aid of two crutches and in quite a lot of pain. John's transfer to a nursing home and slow movement on the extension to the house would at least give me time to get my hip sorted.

During John's stay in hospital I had to take over all his usual roles around the house. We used to say that we worked to our own strengths, me the household activities and him the more cerebral ones! I also had to take charge of the finances which had always been his area. It was very upsetting to see his retirement lump sum being used to fund his nursing home care when ideally we should have been enjoying more time indulging our hobbies and having more than the usual one holiday per year. It was hard to see the car being sold but what was the point of keeping it? I certainly wasn't going to start (or restart) learning to drive now. Fortunately Alan took care of this for us.

It was the little changes in domestic routine that seemed so strange. It was shared responsibility to check that the front door was locked at night before we went to bed but he was always the one to check it. When it came to the dishwasher, well, he made sure that it was loaded to his satisfaction before washing commenced! Also, every working day he used to stand in one corner of the kitchen eating his breakfast cereals before going to work. The long lie-ins he enjoyed at the weekends........! And so it goes on. All these things had been everyday details and now they had gone, some for ever, others perhaps just till he returned.

Shortly after John moved to Cuerden Grange I had a visit from the community occupational therapist, Joanne. We discussed the house extension and how much floor space would be required to make it a room for John which would include a wet room. We arranged a visit from a representative from Anchor Staying Put to see what they could offer. They deliver the Disabilities Facility Grant on behalf of the local authority and can arrange for the work to be carried out by local contractors. Unfortunately and unsurprisingly it was confirmed that we were not eligible for this grant. Also, even if we dismantled the garage (before it dismantled itself, it having been in a precarious state for a number of years!) there was barely sufficient space to build a suitably-sized room for John to manoeuvre in his wheelchair and include a small shower area as well. We would also have needed to make various adaptations to the dining area. Planning permission would be needed for this size of extension along with the alterations. I therefore had to consider the possibility of moving from our house into a bungalow which was something neither of us wanted to do.

Meanwhile I had arranged to have my total hip replacement operation on 8th July. My sister Chris had very kindly offered to come and look after me. Thanks, sis! It is impossible to be at home on your own following this procedure. There are major physical limitations for at least six weeks and Rachael needed to be at work during the day. It was quite a post-op highlight to have John visit me in hospital for a change! I was discharged after six days and was

143

soon able to resume my visits on crutches to Cuerden Grange.

John was slowly able to sit out of bed in his wheelchair for longer periods. We were getting very close to him being able to come home on short visits. Joanne the OT arranged for a platform with removable ramps to be fitted at the front door. So in August he made his first trip home. Now that was an unreal moment!

September brought more ups and downs. Shingles; the great news that he was in remission from the myeloma and then a chest infection! Poor John. He was not able to celebrate the fact that the myeloma was in remission because of all the discomfort and pain from such a severe dose of shingles. During this time I made several enquiries at local estate agencies about the possibility of any bungalows being for sale in the area. There was nothing that looked remotely suitable until I spotted one whilst looking online. This was across the park from us. It had disabled access at the rear and the master bedroom had an en suite bathroom. The photos looked impressive so I arranged a viewing. What a disappointment! It needed quite a lot of work doing to it, especially the kitchen. The bedroom was very dark due to the fact that the en suite was an addition and this had reduced the available natural light. It was overlooked at the back as well. Back to the drawing board!

John recommenced the home visits when the shingles became less painful and continued with the exercises that Gill the physio had given him. The use of the banana board which enabled him to transfer from wheelchair to other seating was to signal the beginning of a whole new chapter in his life. Another unreal moment – John back in his reclining chair! He also stood at the kitchen sink for just a few seconds. Although his posture wasn't good, he was at least weight bearing. I know that on many occasions it was hard for him to return to Cuerden having sampled the delights of being at home. My thanks go to our army of 'pushers' and when he could transfer to a car seat, the drivers who enabled these visits to go ahead.

I don't think that either of us could believe what was happening when it was decided by all present at a meeting in our home in December that John could come home permanently and in time for Christmas! We are so indebted to Joanne the OT who pulled out all the stops to make this happen. I even had a phone call from her at seven o'clock one evening to inform me of the latest developments!

The following few days were all a bit of a blur. So many different feelings. It would be wonderful to have him home but what a responsibility! Would I be able to manage my new 'caring' role? How unusual it was going to be with him sleeping in the dining room and having strangers coming into the house in a morning to get him up, washed and dressed. There was so much to do in those few days as well as preparing for Christmas. The dining table was dispatched to the garage and the hospital bed arrived during a snowstorm! When all the equipment arrived I began to wonder whether there was going to be enough space for all of us.

At last he was back home. Such a momentous occasion and what a splendid Christmas we had Christopher and Alison came for Christmas dinner which we had to eat on lap trays in the lounge! Every time I cooked I had to wheel the stand-aid out of the kitchen and it was difficult to use the back door because that was the only place the sani-chair would fit.

Yes, I was a little anxious about my new role. The district nurse had made sure that I was competent in administering John's daily injection and I was solely in charge of his many medications. We had lots of visitors to the house and my days were quite full. Apart from running the household other jobs included the ordering of repeat inscriptions, arranging hospital transport for clinic appointments, arranging home visits by the phlebotomist and podiatrist and generally looking after John. This involved anything from assisting with toileting, helping him to get undressed at night and general supervision.

I quite enjoyed having the carers in the house as it turned out but when John's progress took such a leap forward (almost literally) we decided that we could cope on our own. Once John could manage the stairs there was no reason why he shouldn't sleep upstairs in our bed but without the air mattress. I had changed from sleeping on the left hand side of the bed (something I had done all our married life) to sleeping on the other side following my hip operation. I had remained on that side simply because things were more accessible. So once he moved upstairs, back to the other side I went – know your place, girl! We also had a stairlift fitted for the days when climbing the stairs was too tiring (for him, that is, not me!).

Of course there were also the visits to Blackpool Victoria Hospital for discussions about High Dose Chemotherapy with Stem Cell Transplant. The harvesting of the stem cells led to yet another hiccough when John's blood pressure took a nosedive. Fortunately they had retrieved sufficient stem cells in the one sitting so he didn't need a repeat performance the following day. These stem cells have been frozen and are being stored in a Liverpool hospital.

We were very excited when our first grandchild, Charlie was born to Alison and Christopher in May 2010. At the time I didn't realise just what a positive impact this gorgeous little one was going to have on our lives. He is just the tonic that John needs and brightens up our world with every visit. At 21 months old he is now taking his grandad for walks around the house. What joy!

John has continued to attempt new challenges. It started with trips to football matches, meals out, cinema and theatre visits, local walks with and without a companion, use of the electric scooter in the local supermarket and short bus journeys. We have experienced the overnight ferry from Hull to Rotterdam spending the following day in Amsterdam and returning again to Hull on the overnight ferry. Last summer we enjoyed a four-day coach holiday to the Cotswolds. He coped admirably last August when Christopher and Alison got married. On a practical note, for quite some time now he's been making cups of coffee, snacks and the occasional simple meal (especially if it contains fish which I hate having to cook!) and even trips up into the loft! Will it ever end? I sincerely hope not!